ANATOMY OF A

LABOR ARBITRATION

by **SAM KAGEL**

A BNA BOOK

BNA Incorporated   Washington 7, D. C.

Printed in the United States of America

Library of Congress Catalog Card Number: 61-10554

20

CONTENTS

PREFACE

This volume is a "How To Do It" book concerned with the preparation and presentation of grievance arbitrations. It is written for all types of persons who engage in this work. For the non-lawyer and lawyer; for the union steward and business agent; for the supervisor, personnel manager and industrial relations director.

This is not a technical book. The problems exposed and examined occur daily in arbitration practice. Of course, not all the subjects considered necessarily develop in a single case. Many problems were telescoped in the discharge case, which forms the core of this book, in order to indicate how they arise in practice and to permit examination of all of them within the framework of the case.

This book reflects some thirty years experience of the author in the field of industrial relations; as an advocate, teacher, and currently as an arbitrator. The suggestions made herein as to practice and procedure are based on this experience. Others may, of course, have different, but equally valid, points of view on the problems considered in this book.

Labor arbitration is a relatively new field with room for differing opinions as to practice and procedure. Most important is the need to maintain the integrity of the arbitration process. This is the responsibility of the advocate. He can accomplish this in large measure by learning and improving the techniques of preparing and presenting arbitration cases.

This volume was read in draft form by a group of advocates representing both unions and employers. Many of their suggestions were incorporated in the final draft. To them, I acknowledge with thanks their helpfulness and interest.

This book could not have been completed without the monumental aid of Virginia B. Smith, my law office associate. Many of her excellent suggestions are incorporated in this volume. Most of the research reflected in the appendices is her work. For all this, she has my profound thanks.

Finally, I acknowledge my gratitude to my wife, who, during the past years, shared the burden of my work. This constituted a most positive aid in writing this volume.

Of course, for the record, it must be written that this book, its contents and conclusions, are solely my own responsibility.

Sam Kagel.

San Francisco, California
January 3, 1961

INTRODUCTION

Over twenty million workers in the United States have their wages, hours, and working conditions determined by collective bargaining. And several million other workers, not covered by collective bargaining agreements, are affected by the employment terms established through labor-management negotiation.

The primary objective of the collective bargaining process is the *settlement of differences* between employees and employers concerning the terms and conditions of their work relationship. In labor-management relations this process of collective bargaining, after the matter of representation is settled, arises at two points:

1. deciding upon the terms of the collective bargaining agreement.

2. settling disputes arising during the term of the agreement.

The agreement itself provides only the skeleton, the bare bones of collective bargaining. It is the day-to-day settlement of disputes arising during the life of the agreement that provides the flesh and blood of collective bargaining.

Labor unions and employers have devised various techniques for carrying on collective bargaining; that is, the process of settling their differences. The techniques include:

1. *negotiation:* meeting together, by themselves, and through discussion arriving at a mutually acceptable settlement of the dispute.

2. *conciliation and mediation:* bringing a disinterested third person into the discussions between the parties. The third person has no authority to decide the dispute. His purpose is to help the parties in any way he can to reach their own settlement of the dispute.

3. *economic action:* attempting by direct economic pressure and power to influence the other party's decision on the disputed

issue. It can take many forms such as strike, lockout, boycott, picketing and variations or combinations of these.

4. *legal action:* obtaining injunctions, filing unfair labor practice charges with the National Labor Relations Board, filing damage suits, or using other legal devices to affect the respective bargaining positions of the union and employer.

5. *arbitration:* giving a disinterested third person the authority to render a final and binding decision on the dispute.

6. *political action:* seeking to influence the legislative and executive actions of government as they affect labor legislation and its administration.

In arriving at the terms of the agreement, all of the above techniques may be used, separately or in combination with one another. How well the methods are used depends upon the skill and knowledge of the bargaining representatives.

In settling grievances, that is disputes, arising during the term of the agreement, only two of the techniques are ordinarily used, negotiation and arbitration. Rarely, if ever, is conciliation or mediation used at this point; nor is direct political action ordinarily involved in the settlement of grievance disputes. In many instances, the parties have given up their rights to use direct economic force by including no-strike and no-lockout clauses in their agreements. If the dispute involves an unfair labor practice or gives rise to a legal cause of action, the parties may use legal action, but its use is limited.

Most collective bargaining agreements provide machinery for the purpose of settling disputes arising during the term of an agreement. These grievance procedures take many forms, but ordinarily the first three or four steps use the *negotiation* technique at progressively higher levels of authority in the company and the union. In these steps the parties themselves, through oral discussion, try to settle the dispute. The final step of these procedures usually provides for *arbitration*. At that step the parties say "We can't settle it. Let's bring in somebody from the outside and have him tell us what to do. We will agree in advance to accept his decision as final and binding."

This book is concerned with only one of the methods of labor-management dispute settlement: arbitration and primarily as it is used in grievance arbitration. At the outset of our discussion of this technique, certain underlying principles should be stated:

1. The best way to settle a dispute—any dispute—is by *negotiation*. Most disputes are, in fact, settled in this way.

2. Arbitration should be the last resort for the parties, in the same way that courts should be used as the last resort in a legal controversy.

3. Arbitration should never be used as a substitute for negotiation; nor should it be used, except in rare instances, as a device to "save face."

Because arbitration is widely used as the terminal step in grievance procedures, literally thousands of labor and management representatives have had to learn about the process. For many of them, arbitration was a new and confusing way to settle disputes. Undoubtedly, the best way to learn about a new technique is to become involved in it. But opportunities for such a slow (and perhaps costly) growth of skill and knowledge are not always available. The very first arbitration case in which a business agent, union or employer counsel, or management representative is involved may be a case that requires considerable knowledge and skill to satisfactorily handle the dispute.

Perhaps the next best thing to actual experience in arbitration is to sit in on a case and watch its development. This book is an attempt to provide that experience; to let you sit in on a grievance arbitration case, to sit in while the parties to a case are determining whether there is actually an arbitrable issue, to look on while the personnel officer is discussing a grievance with the company attorney, to hear the union counsel and the company attorney make preparations for the case, and finally to be a spectator at the arbitration hearing itself. But this will be more than a mere demonstration of a case; it will be a vivisection. The example case will be taken apart and its elements examined. Through this process some ground rules will be developed for those who are involved in the arbitration of grievances and valuable insight will be given into the grievance process for those who deal with grievances at any step in the settlement procedure.

The example case concerns Mrs. Green. Let it be conceded right now that it is "loaded" in her favor. And that many management representatives would never permit this grievance to go to arbitration. But her case has the virtue of simplicity, and therefore lends itself to an uncomplicated and easier study of the anatomy of a labor arbitration.

The use of arbitration is, of course, not limited to the settlement of labor-management disputes. As the courts become more crowded and business problems become more technical, the use of commercial arbitration grows. To some extent what is said in this book will be helpful to those engaged in any type of arbitration. But the primary focus of the book is on labor-management arbitration, and more specifically the arbitration of grievances arising under a collective bargaining agreement.

CHAPTER I

WHAT IS A GRIEVANCE FOR PURPOSES OF ARBITRATION

What is a grievance? There's no easy general answer to this question. The following conversation between a worker and his shop steward will indicate a few of the factors that determine whether a complaint is the kind of grievance that comes within the agreement, or just a complaint for which the agreement provides no relief.

> The "worker" has just buttonholed his "shop steward."
>
> WORKER: My foreman is a bum. Every day he gets to be more of a bum.
>
> STEWARD: So what?
>
> WORKER: Well, you're the shop steward, aren't you? I want you to do something about it. He's a bum, and I can prove it.
>
> STEWARD: So you can prove it. I can't do anything about it. Tell him.
>
> WORKER: Look, we've got a collective bargaining agreement with the company, haven't we?
>
> STEWARD: Sure.
>
> WORKER: Well, it gives us a right to make complaints, doesn't it? And we have a grievance procedure, don't we?
>
> STEWARD: Yes, but just because you think your boss is a bum doesn't necessarily mean we have a grievance coming under the terms of the agreement.
>
> WORKER: If you worked with him you'd think it was a grievance.

1

STEWARD: Maybe you'd better tell me what you mean. Does he do anything on the job that violates our contract?

WORKER: I suppose not. He's too smart for that. But he's a real so-and-so. The way he orders you around, the way he looks at you. He's just plain miserable!

The complaint must come within the terms of the agreement

STEWARD: There's nothing in the agreement which says he can't be miserable or be a bum. Now, if his actions as a so-and-so violate the agreement then you would have a grievance which arises out of our agreement with the company. And we could try and cut him down to size. But unless he does something which provides you with a complaint under the terms of our agreement, there's nothing we can do about your beef.

WORKER: We should change our agreement. Couldn't we include in the agreement that any complaint should be treated as a grievance?

STEWARD: I suppose so. But I'm still not certain it would help in this case. Some agreements do provide that any dissatisfaction of a worker that is related to his work situation or his employment relationship is a grievance. I don't know whether your complaint is related to the work situation. When you say he's a bum, are you talking about him as a person?

WORKER: Of course. He's just that kind of a guy. He'd be a bum anywhere.

STEWARD: That doesn't sound to me like a complaint related to your job. Even if we had broader language in the agreement, I don't think we'd get anywhere trying to call that a grievance.

As the shop steward points out, not all worker grievances are grievances within the meaning of the particular agreement involved. To determine whether an employer or employee complaint is a grievance subject to the agreement, it is necessary to first ascertain and understand the facts on which the complaint is based; and second, to analyze the language of the arbitration clause in the collective bargaining agreement with reference to those specific facts.

It should be noted that parties can provide that any worker grievance may be processed through the negotiation steps of the grievance procedure, but that only matters regarding the actual interpretation or application of the written agreement may be taken to arbitration. Such a provision must be clearly stated in the agreement.

At the outset it becomes clear, therefore, that it is the language of the agreement that controls the rights and duties of the parties. Throughout this book, it will be evident that the original drafting of the provisions of the agreement relating to arbitration is of prime importance. Such clauses should not be merely copies from other agreements. They should be "custom tailored" for and by each set of parties to a collective bargaining agreement.

This subject will hereinafter be discussed as it relates to various problems that arise from the arbitration process.

COMMENT: See Appendix A for a general and detailed discussion of the problems involved in drafting arbitration clauses.

CHAPTER II

IS THE DISPUTE ARBITRABLE

If the parties can't settle a grievance by negotiation, one or the other may consider the possibility of going to arbitration. Having failed to settle the argument, he says, in effect, "Let's turn it over to someone else and let him decide it for us." Such a decision should be made only after the moving party has carefully weighed several considerations.

Arbitration is not always the best solution when the parties fail to settle a grievance by negotiation. In some instances it may be better to withdraw the grievance. Many of the considerations that should influence the decision to take a dispute to arbitration will be discussed in the next chapter.

But even before that determination, there is one basic question which must be answered by anyone considering arbitrating a dispute: *Is the dispute arbitrable?* Under the general arbitration clauses of the controlling collective bargaining agreement, or under the terms of a special arbitration agreement, is this particular dispute one on which the arbitrator has the power to render a valid and binding decision? Put another way: Have the parties given authority to someone else to decide the issues involved in the dispute?

The following conversation will illustrate how the issue of arbitrability could arise. The same conversation can occur between either union representatives or employer representatives. Both union and employer spokesmen should carefully weigh the points and problems discussed in the illustration.

The conversation involves a situation in which the union referred a dispute on wages arising out of a wage-reopening clause to the grievance procedure in the agreement. The parties considered the dispute under this procedure. But when the union requested arbitration, the employer claimed that the subject matter in dispute was not arbitrable under the terms of the agreement.

COUNSEL: Before I'm able to give you any kind of advice, I will have to take a look at your agreement. Did you bring a copy?

UNION: Yes. Here it is.

COUNSEL: Now, I assume you're referring to this Section 32. It looks to me like there are two sections that apply, both 32 and 33. Section 33 is the one that provides for the wage reopening, as I recall.

Yes, here it is. It's a two-year agreement and provides that wages may be reopened after the first year for the purpose of amendment, and that's all it provides. Then Section 32 reads: "Disputes arising between the parties during the term of this agreement shall be submitted to an adjustment board and if the adjustment board is unable to agree, then the dispute shall be settled by arbitration."

Is that the section you are referring to?

UNION: Yes.

COUNSEL: Is that what you relied upon when you asked for arbitration?

UNION: Yes, sure. There's another clause in there that says we can't strike, isn't there?

COUNSEL: Yes, that's right. There's a no-strike clause.

UNION: Well, I figured if we couldn't settle with them, we'd arbitrate the matter. Now they tell us we can't arbitrate, and the agreement tells us we can't strike.

COUNSEL: It looks like we have one of those tough questions on arbitrability.

UNION: What do you mean — tough question? They haven't got a leg to stand on, have they? Don't we have an agreement to arbitrate?

COUNSEL: Yes, we do. But your employer will probably argue that even though there is an agreement to arbitrate, the interim wage issue isn't the kind of dispute that comes under the arbitration clause.

UNION: How can he do that? The agreement says 'disputes,' and this is a dispute.

COUNSEL: He would probably argue that this isn't the kind of dispute usually handled through the grievance procedure and that the arbitration agreement only refers to disputes having to do with the interpretation of the agreement. Not to make a new agreement term, such as setting a new wage.

Power of arbitrator

As you know, the arbitrator gets his power, authority, or jurisdiction to make a final and binding decision only from the mutual consent or joint agreement of the parties.

UNION: Suppose management refuses to arbitrate. What can we do?

Decision on arbitrability

COUNSEL: Well, we can see if they will agree to let the arbitrator decide whether the dispute is arbitrable. Or we might have to go into court to try to obtain an order directing the employer to arbitrate. We can do that in our state. Of course, the court might find that there is no agreement to arbitrate at all.

COMMENT: Appendix C sets forth current law in the states and territories relative to enforceability of agreements to arbitrate and enforcement of arbitration awards.

UNION: Which is better—to go to court or to let an arbitrator decide whether it's arbitrable?

COUNSEL: If we can get the employer to agree, I'd rather leave it up to the arbitrator. We could handle the matter more quickly, and an arbitrator would have a greater understanding than the court of the practical situation involved in collective bargaining relationships.

UNION: **All right.** I'll report all this to my executive committee and then get in touch with you again.

Now let us summarize the problem of arbitrability. The question of whether or not a dispute is arbitrable constantly arises. To determine arbitrability, it is necessary to distinguish clearly among at least the following three situations:

1. An issue of arbitrability arises when one of the parties argues that the dispute in question *is not within the scope of the arbitration* agreement and that an arbitrator would not have the power or jurisdiction to render a final and binding award.

What is meant by the "scope of the agreement to arbitrate" is controlled by the language of the arbitration clause in the agreement. Suppose the clause provides that "only disputes arising out of the interpretation or application of the agreement" are subject to arbitration. Then clearly a dispute seeking to add a completely new provision to the agreement would not be arbitrable. Suppose the clause reads that "any and all disputes between the parties arising during the life of the agreement shall be arbitrated." Then it is evident that even a new provision could be added to the agreement through grievance arbitration. Or at least this could be argued. (See Appendix A.)

2. In the second situation, a party claims that there is *no agreement* which requires them to arbitrate.

This is not a true issue of "arbitrability," but is often referred to in this way. In this case, the contention of one of the parties is that he is not bound by any agreement to arbitrate anything. This type of dispute in which the existence of an arbitration agreement is questioned must ordinarily be settled by a court in accordance with applicable law, unless the parties specifically give an arbitrator the authority to settle such a question. The issue to be settled by court or arbitrator is whether or not there is *any agreement* to arbitrate.

    3. In the third situation, the parties have agreed to arbitrate a particular dispute but are unable to agree upon a statement of the issue.

Again, this is not a true issue of "arbitrability" but is often confused with such a question. In this situation neither party is denying the existence of an agreement to arbitrate. They also agree that the particular dispute is subject to arbitration and that they are bound to arbitrate the dispute. *But they cannot agree on how to state the issue.*

The disagreement on how to state the issue may arise because one party or the other is insisting upon a "loaded" statement of the issue. For example: "Was there just cause to discharge John Jones after he hit the foreman who swore at him and pushed him?" This statement includes the position of one of the parties. It assumes facts and makes conclusions. In short, it not only includes the question to be decided but it also includes a statement of the position of one of the parties.

There is a single test to apply to separate out the issue from contentions of the parties. The test is: What question or questions do you want the arbitrator to answer? In the example given, the question to be answered by the arbitrator is: "Was John Jones discharged for just cause?"

The statement that the foreman swore and pushed Jones is what the union apparently intends to argue as an excuse for Jones. But this position of the union and the contentions of the company, whatever they may be, are what will have to be placed in evidence at the hearing. And it is the arbitrator's function to weigh this evidence in order to determine whether or not there was just cause for the discharge.

Therefore, the statement of the issue must be an objective statement; a statement that does not include as a conclusion the claim, or part of the claim, made by either party. If the parties cannot agree on a statement of the issue, the arbitrator can sometimes assist the parties to state the issue. Because the wording of the issue submitted to the arbitrator goes to the very heart of his jurisdiction and authority, the importance of its being clearly stated cannot be overemphasized.

COMMENT: There is a further illustration of this problem in Chapter V, *The Submission Agreement*. In that situation the parties, although initially in disagreement over how to state the issue, eventually were able to negotiate the matter and to agree upon the statement of it prior to going to arbitration.

Who decides arbitrability

The facts of many labor-management disputes could give rise to an issue of arbitrability. It is difficult to draft an agreement in such a way as to completely eliminate the possibility of a dispute as to arbitrability. Recognizing this, some parties have provided in their agreement that any issue of arbitrability shall be submitted to the arbitrator for his decision. Even in the absence of such an agreement, this issue is usually submitted by the parties to the arbitrator for his decision, although in some states the courts have held that the issue of arbitrability is for the courts to determine unless the parties have specifically agreed otherwise. But in some situations, the parties themselves prefer to have the issue determined by the courts.

The United States Supreme Court, and the federal appellate courts have ruled on this issue in several recent cases. The cases were concerned with the right of enforcement of arbitration clauses in collective bargaining agreements and arose under Sec. 301 of the Taft-Hartley Act. In these 1960 cases, the Supreme Court held that in the first instance the court must determine whether a particular controversy comes within the scope of the arbitration agreement unless the parties have submitted that question to the arbitrator. But the Court cautioned judges exercising this function not to overstep their limits. They were directed not to go into the merits of the controversy under the guise of deciding whether or not it was within the scope of the agreement. In addition the court was cautioned that if a dispute is arbitrable within the terms of the agreement the court can not refuse arbitration on the basis that the moving party is wrong on his claim.

A Court of Appeals decision held that it was also for the courts to determine, in the first instance, the question of procedural arbitrability unless the parties had submitted it to the arbitrator. The question of procedural arbitrability involves questions of whether procedural steps which the agreement requires prior to arbitration have been taken within the proper time.

COMMENT: See Appendix C for a note on the legal problem of who shall decide the issue of arbitrability— the arbitrator or the court. The court decisions noted above are reproduced in Appendix D.

The important item to remember is that the language of the arbitration clause, depending on whether it is narrowly or broadly drawn, will control the initial determination as to arbitrability.

One further point on this question of arbitrability should be mentioned. Some arbitrators have held that the parties must raise the issue of arbitrability at one of the grievance procedure steps prior to the arbitration hearing. If this is required, it may hamper efforts to settle the grievance through negotiation. Rather than run the risk of losing the right to raise the issue of arbitrability after negotiations have failed (if they do fail), the parties would feel compelled to argue this technicality early in negotiations, thus possibly interfering with genuine attempts to settle the dispute without resorting to arbitration.

Other arbitrators, following what seems to be the better view, permit the issue of arbitrability to be raised for the first time at the hearing. Because this issue is crucial only if the parties do, in fact, resort to arbitration, the right to raise it for the first time at the hearing places neither party at a disadvantage and yet has the positive value of freeing the negotiation steps from unnecessary technicalities.

Because questions concerning arbitrability are the source of so much confusion, a method of analysis is suggested here. The parties should consider their situation in terms of four questions. These questions, and their effect on arbitrability are shown in the chart below. Note that in column A the parties have asked only the first question; in column B the first two questions, etc.

	A	B	C	D
1st Question	Is there an agreement between the parties to arbitrate? If answer is YES	Answer to question 1 is YES.	Answer to question 1 is YES.	Answer to question 1 is YES.
2nd Question		Does the particular problem involved come within the scope of the agreement? If answer is YES	Answer to question 2 is YES.	Answer to question 2 is YES.
3rd question			Have all the procedural steps required by the arbitration agreement been taken in proper time or waived? If answer is YES	Answer to question 3 is YES.
4th Question				Has the *statement* of the issue been agreed upon? YES or NO
CONCLUSION	A YES answer only is not enough to conclude that a particular dispute is arbitrable. See Column B	A YES answer to questions 1 and 2 make it possible to tentatively conclude that a dispute is arbitrable *unless* the answer to question 3 is NO. See Column C	A YES answer to questions 1, 2, and 3 establishes that the dispute is arbitrable. *But* note possible effect of question 4. See Column D	If answer is YES dispute is arbitrable. If answer is NO, the right to arbitrate remains, but the problem of status of the issue remains to be settled by the parties or by reference to the arbitrator.

CHECKLIST: ARBITRABILITY

When confronted with a possible problem as to arbitrability the parties should ask themselves the following questions:

1. Is there in existence any *agreement* to arbitrate? If this question is in dispute, then ordinarily it is a matter for the courts to decide. (Though the parties could agree, if they desire, to submit such a question to an arbitrator for decision.)

2. Is there a dispute as to whether a particular dispute comes under an arbitration agreement even though both parties agree that they are bound to arbitrate?

If this is the nature of the dispute, then the parties should further explore:

— the language of the arbitration agreement.

— the nature of the particular dispute.

— whether there is any express or implied agreement to submit issues of arbitrability to an arbitrator, if no general agreement to do so exists.

— the federal law, the law of the state or territory as to who (the arbitrator or the court) has authority to determine an issue of arbitrability in the absence of an express agreement that the arbitrator shall have the authority.

Chapter III

SHOULD THE DISPUTE GO TO ARBITRATION

When a grievance has been processed through all the negotiation steps of the procedure without being settled, the parties must consider whether or not they should take the dispute to arbitration. And while most collective bargaining agreements provide arbitration as the terminal step in the grievance procedure, it should not be resorted to automatically. In fact, many cases go to arbitration that should have been dropped before that stage—even though they hadn't been finally settled.

Assuming the dispute is clearly arbitrable, what do the parties need to know to decide whether they should go to arbitration? They should consider at least all of the following:

— what kind of a case does the complaining party have, is it strong or weak?

— does the case include a general principle which must be decided because of the possibility of other similar fact situations arising?

— is the dispute important enough to justify the cost of arbitration?

— is there a satisfactory arbitrator available for the kind of dispute involved?

— what will be the consequences of various possible decisions — (don't always assume the arbitrator will give you the decision).

— is this the kind of case in which the complaining party could "win the argument but lose the battle"? (i.e. What will be the effect on future labor relations and on negotiations of future agreements? A favorable decision on one dispute may raise additional problems that outweigh the value of the single victory.)

— is the issue something which could be taken up more effectively during agreement negotiations?

14

The following two conversations (1) between an employer attorney and personnel manager and (2) between a union representative and a local official will illustrate factors that the parties to a dispute should ordinarily consider in order to decide whether or not they should go to arbitration. The case they are considering involves a grievance that the union and management were unable to successfully settle in the negotiation steps of the grievance procedure.

> Pers. Manager: We've got trouble at one of our stores.
>
> Counsel: So.
>
> Pers. Manager: Yes, we've got a lady clerk, Mrs. Green, down at the Z grocery store who we claim quit. Now the union has put in a complaint and claims that we discharged her. On top of that, she's claiming that her May pay check should have included sick leave payments for the time she was sick last month.
>
> We've tried to settle this thing with the union, but we aren't getting anywhere. The union wants to go to arbitration. What do we do now?
>
> COMMENT: Disputes that arise during the life of the agreement are generally of two kinds: (1) interpretation of agreement language, that is the facts are agreed to but the parties cannot determine how to apply them to the agreement (the sick leave claim is an example of this). (2) a fact issue involving the application of agreement terms. That is the facts are in dispute so that arbitrator must sift the facts and apply them to the agreement (the issue of whether the clerk quit or was discharged is the latter type).
>
> Counsel: I'll need to look at the agreement covering your store before we do anything else. Do you have a copy with you?
>
> Pers. Manager: No. I didn't bring down the agreement. I don't have an extra copy of it but I had my secretary knock out a copy of a couple of the sections and here they are.

Agreement must be read as a whole

COUNSEL: I appreciate that, but I'm going to have to see the entire agreement.

PERS. MANAGER: Why? This gives us the clauses involved; the sick leave provision, and the clause giving the discharge procedure—but we don't even need that one because we didn't discharge her.

COUNSEL: Well, if you've interpreted the agreement so well, I don't know why you're coming to me. If you want me to help you, I have to see the entire agreement, not just what you think is pertinent in the agreement. Often the agreement has other provisions which may apply or be related to the dispute. I'm not going to even consider the case unless I have the entire agreement and can analyze it from all four corners to see what I think is relevant or applies to the issues.

I haven't all the facts yet, but first of all I want the entire agreement, not just those two sections.

PERS. MANAGER: All right. I'll have to get it. It's the only copy I've got but I'll get it for you. I'll be glad to send it down.

COUNSEL: Be sure and do that. That is the key document. I want to study it.

COMMENT: The practice that an agreement should be read from "all four corners," i.e., each and every provision of the agreement, cannot be over-emphasized. Arbitrators have sometimes found that after a case had been submitted and the arbitrator had occasion to study the agreement, certain provisions of the agreement which had been overlooked by both parties, either affect the case as presented, or in some instances would have settled the dispute without need to go to arbitration.

In addition to that I will also want some of the preceding agreements for maybe the three or four years preceding the present agreement.

PERS. MANAGER: What for?

History of development of provisions

COUNSEL: Well, you have a dispute here of some kind and apparently the agreement provisions are applicable. I'd like to know just how the agreement provisions developed and——

PERS. MANAGER: I don't think these sections have changed at all.

Examine all documents

COUNSEL: Well, I appreciate your "thinking" on that, but I want to be sure they didn't change, so I'd like the agreements for at least four years back.

And also I want copies of any exchange of letters between you and the union on these disputes. Were there any letters on it?

PERS. MANAGER: Yes.

COUNSEL: Do you have any copies with you?

PERS. MANAGER: No.

COUNSEL: Well, I'll need them, so bring them along when you bring the agreements. Now, you said you met with the union on this. Are there any minutes or reports on those meetings?

PERS. MANAGER: I think so, but I'll have to check with the office to be sure.

Grievance file

COUNSEL: Bring along whatever you have in writing on it. And also, if she filed a formal grievance, I'll want to look at that too. In order to advise you on this matter, I must examine all these documents. Any one of them might include crucial material.

PERS. MANAGER: Okay. You'll get them.

COMMENT: It is of the utmost importance that a complete file be kept of every grievance. Such file should include copies of the current agreement; any expired agreements which may be relevant to the dispute; copies of the written complaint and any written answers to the complaint; all correspondence dealing with the dispute.

Official minutes of adjustment or grievance board meetings should be provided for. Such minutes should be approved by appropriate signatures of the parties, before being considered as the official minutes. In the absence of official minutes, the parties should make and retain complete and accurate notes of the proceedings at such meetings.

Get the facts

COUNSEL: Now that we've got that out of the way, let's consider the sick leave pay claim first. What are the facts on that?

PERS. MANAGER: Last month she was out the 1st, 2nd, 3rd and 4th. The 1st was a Friday, and she came back to work on Tuesday.

The agreement says we pay sick leave if the sick leave extends beyond a 3-day period. We claim that means three working days and the union is claiming it means three calendar days.

COUNSEL: I see. You're agreed on the facts then?

PERS. MANAGER: Yes.

Understand the issue

COUNSEL: And the problem is that she was sick for only two scheduled work days but for four calendar days.

PERS. MANAGER: That's it exactly. The language is clearly in our favor.

COUNSEL: Well, if it's so clear, why the argument between you and the union? You tell me the agreement provides for sick leave after a three-day period. Does it read three calendar days or three working days?

PERS. MANAGER: Neither, it just says three days.

COUNSEL: That's the point. The language is not clear. It's ambiguous. It could mean either one.

PERS. MANAGER: Well, how do we clear it up for the arbitrator?

COUNSEL: If we can convince the arbitrator that the language is ambiguous, then he should allow us to put in evidence of "past practice," and, if it would help clarify its meaning, evidence on the negotiation history of that clause.

Use of past practice, and history of negotiations

COMMENT: If a party can establish his claim that the language is unclear or ambiguous, then he should introduce past practice and the history of negotiations if they support his interpretation of the language. The purpose of this evidence is to aid the arbitrator in resolving the ambiguity. And the manner in which the parties have applied the language in the past is a good key to what they intend the language to mean.

Weight would be given to the past practice in interpreting the language of the provision, if the practice remained reasonably constant before and after negotiations in which one of the parties had proposed, but failed to obtain, a change in the language of the provision. And the very existence of an opportunity to negotiate a change in the clause, even though neither party chose to do so, would lend some weight to the contention that past practice was consistent with the meaning that the parties gave to the language in the agreement.

Many times both parties will claim that the language is *not* ambiguous. Each will argue that it is very clear, that is, if his view of the agreement is adopted. In such instances the arbitrator if, in fact, he believes the language is not clear, should ask for past practice, if any, and the history of negotiations on this provision. Such evidence may help the arbitrator determine the intent of the parties.

COUNSEL: Let's leave the sick leave issue then until I have a chance to look at the agreement and other documents. And get me the past practice and history of negotiations on the sick leave provision. Maybe we can agree to submit this issue by briefs. That would save some expense. What about the discharge problem?

PERS. MANAGER: We didn't fire the lady. She quit.

Interview the witnesses

COUNSEL: How do you know that? Were you present when the incident occurred that led up to this grievance?

PERS. MANAGER: No. You know I have to cover fifteen stores in this area. I wasn't there when it happened, but Red—he's the manager—was there and he told me everything that happened. He told me that this lady just picked up her coat and quit. And then she came back the next day ready to go to work. Red told her then that he couldn't use her because he had hired somebody else. And then Red told her she was going to be discharged anyway for not following store rules.

COUNSEL: I certainly want to interview Red and get all the information I can from him.

PERS. MANAGER: You mean I've got to take him off the job? You know I've only got a couple of clerks and a manager on at that store. If I take Red off, it doesn't matter what day, it's pretty rough. And he'll start screaming if I ask him to come down on his day off.

COMMENT: There is no substitute for getting the facts "first-hand." To get the information from any other "second-hand" source may lead to distortion. The distortion may result from forgetting and misinterpretation, but in many situations the witness may hold back some of the facts, or color them somewhat if he is telling the story to his immediate supervisor. After all, if the witness was involved in the dispute, he's on the spot too. And even in interviews with the witness himself, facts may be colored or forgotten for the moment if the supervisor of the witness is present. If witnesses are interviewed privately and separately the advocate has a far greater chance of getting a frank, complete, and honest statement. This is essential to better judge the merits of the case and to properly plan its presentation.

COUNSEL: Well, that's up to you. I'd prefer to have him in my office. Then, if I want to, I can have my secretary take down his statement.

PERS. MANAGER: He told me what happened. I can tell you. Don't you want to hear the story?

Witness: importance of selecting

COUNSEL: I know, but it won't do any good. I'd like to get the general story from you just for the purpose of analyzing your agreement when I get it, but it's Red who will be the witness at the hearing. Not you.

PERS. MANAGER: You mean you're going to have to use him as a witness?

Problem of hearsay

COUNSEL: I certainly will. He's going to tell what happened. Only Red can testify to the facts. All you can testify to is what he told you were the facts and that would be hearsay. The union won't let us get by with that. They will want the man who was on the scene at the time so they can cross-examine him.

PERS. MANAGER: Okay. I'll have to arrange for that, too, then.

COMMENT: Hearsay evidence testimony is given by a person who "heard someone else say (thus hearsay) something." It is not something that he, the witness himself heard or viewed. It is "second-hand" evidence. Since hearsay is "second-hand" it is generally given less weight than would be given evidence testified to by the original speaker or actor. This does not mean that the witness giving the hearsay evidence is not to be believed. But he is once or more removed from the original utterance of the words in question or from the action involved in the incident in question.

A witness is put on the stand to tell his story. The other party and the arbitrator can test his recollection and credibility by "sizing him up" (this is called observing his demeanor) and by cross-examination. Clearly these methods are inapplicable when used with the one who "heard someone else say" something. It is the "someone else" who would be the best witness.

As a general rule, hearsay evidence is not allowed in a court trial. Courts usually require the original witness be brought in to testify. But if this is impossible, the court must determine whether, as a matter of necessity and as an exception to the general rule, the hearsay evidence can be admitted. Thus the right to introduce hearsay evidence must be argued in each case. Although it continues to be a bothersome technicality, the courts have substantially limited the effect of the hearsay rule by establishing numerous classes of exceptions to the rule, and if counsel can argue that the offered evidence falls into one of these exceptions, the hearsay will be admitted.

In arbitration hearings, the "rule" is more realistic and practical. Hearsay is permitted if it is relevant, but is given less weight than would be given if the original observer were testifying. Hearsay is not as persuasive as original evidence; by its nature there is no opportunity to cross-examine or rebut the substance of the hearsay.

In view of this problem an advocate should, whenever possible, avoid the use of hearsay. He should prepare his case intensively always seeking the original evidence, the primary witness, in short, the best, the strongest evidence to support his case.

COUNSEL: Were there any other witnesses to this incident?

PERS. MANAGER: No, I don't think so. Red would know, but I think it was just between the clerk and the manager.

COUNSEL: As far as you know, where did the incident take place?

PERS. MANAGER: Apparently all over the store. The way I understand it, from what Red told me, he had asked her to wash the front doors. We have those push-in glass doors and the little kids get their hands on them and they get sticky and dirty two or three times a day, so he asked her to wash the glass and she wouldn't do it. She said that under the agreement she didn't have to do that kind of work, that's for the janitor to do. And that led to an argument and——

COUNSEL: Let me stop you there for just a moment.

Was there anyone present when that happened? Did Red say anyone was present?

PERS. MANAGER: He didn't say. I understand the argument was in the back of the store.

COUNSEL: Well, your understanding isn't enough. This is one other point to illustrate why I want to interview Red, to find out whether there were other witnesses to this argument.

PERS. MANAGER: All right. Then they got into this argument in the back of the store and then Red—you know what kind of a guy he is—he's a darn good manager but once in a while he gets excited. But anyway, then he——

COUNSEL: I gather from what you just said he's an excellent store manager but sometimes lacking in good relationships with his personnel.

PERS. MANAGER: You'll see what I mean. You see—

COUNSEL: That's another reason I want to see Red, to find out what kind of a witness he will be, whether he's hot-headed or even tempered or what.

PERS. MANAGER: Well, he's red headed.

COUNSEL: You mean he's inclined to blow up sometimes? We may find that Red's wrong.

PERS. MANAGER: He'd better not be. We can't afford to have him wrong. We're having too much trouble with this union and we might have to back this guy right or wrong.

COUNSEL: Wait a minute. If this is going to be a face-saving arbitration, let's consider it carefully.

Face-saving arbitrations

This is not a matter to be taken lightly. If Red is wrong, is it better to go to arbitration and lose, or is it better to straighten Red out and make him understand the requirements for a normal, intelligent employee relationship?

After I analyze this case and make a recommendation as to whether we have or have not a good case to bring to arbitration, I want you to really consider this matter carefully. I want you to weigh the possibility of losing the arbitration. Sometimes the consequences of winning or losing are very serious matters.

> COMMENT: It is recognized that at times so-called "face-saving" arbitrations may be in order. They should not be used, however, solely because one or the other of the parties is afraid to tell those that he represents that they are wrong. The attitude that any union member or supervisor "right or wrong" will always be supported is injurious to the union or the employer. And the arbitration process should not be resorted to because a union or employer representative may lack the courage to take a position.

PERS. MANAGER: I see what you mean. We'll talk about that again after you've talked to Red. I can see now why you have to have all this material and why you have to talk to Red himself.

COUNSEL: Experience has taught me that an employee, in talking to a person in charge, like you—you do have the authority to hire and fire employees such as Red, don't you?

PERS. MANAGER: Oh, yes, absolutely.

COUNSEL: This type of employee will quite often tell you a story to cover up his own mistakes. If Red has made a mistake I want to find out about it because if I can't find it out from him in our conference, the union will find it out when we are in the arbitration hearing. We don't want to be taken by surprise. You can see that.

PERS. MANAGER: Yes, you're right. That could be pretty damaging.

COUNSEL: Now, I interrupted your story with respect to the argument in the back of the store.

PERS. MANAGER: Well, Red told Mrs. Green, "Look, we've got a report on you that you were not giving out register slips with the packages." After that, according to Red, she really blew her top and grabbed her coat and ran out of the store, or walked out of the store, I'm not sure which.

We figured she just plain quit, but the union is insisting that she was discharged.

COUNSEL: So the union is going to contend in this case that she was discharged and you are going to contend she quit.

PERS. MANAGER: I guess so. Well, what else did you want from me? I've got to get back on the job.

COUNSEL: You spoke of a report on register slips. What kind of a report was that?

PERS. MANAGER: Well, you know we have the Detective Company that sends around shoppers for us who gives us reports on the clerks. One of the reports said that this Mrs. Green wasn't putting the register tapes from the cash register machines into the packages. She works at one of the check stands.

COUNSEL: I see. Who hired the detective agency?

PERS. MANAGER: I did.

COUNSEL: Do they work solely for you?

PERS. MANAGER: I guess they work for other stores, too.

COUNSEL: Do they go to all your stores?

PERS. MANAGER: Yes, they go to all our stores.

COUNSEL: As I understand it then, this mistake was observed by a shopper from the Detective Company.

PERS. MANAGER: Yes, that's right.

Get facts from primary source COUNSEL: Then I will want to interview that person, too.

PERS. MANAGER: I don't think I can manage that. The agency won't tell who the shopper is. I don't even know myself.

COUNSEL: Then how are we going to prove the incident that occurred with respect to the slips?

PERS. MANAGER: They gave me the report.

Counsel: We'll need that report but that isn't enough.

Pers. Manager: What's the matter with the report? This is a licensed detective outfit.

Use of documents as evidence

Counsel: The union can't cross-examine a written report. They will want to cross-examine the person who saw what actually occurred. I want to have that observer present. At the arbitration, the union may ask that the shopper be present. The union could object to this report going in without a foundation being laid by the person who made it. I need both the shopper who made the report and the report made to the detective agency.

Pers. Manager: I can give you the report.

Counsel: Is that the same as the report the shopper made or did the supervisor of the detective agency make out a report to send to you after reading the shopper's report?

Pers. Manager: I don't know that.

Counsel: Well, we'll have to find out. I will probably need the shopper and whoever made the report that came into your possession, if it was not made directly by the shopper.

Pers. Manager: You make this sound like a felony case. Why do you have to have all these things?

Careful and detailed investigation

Counsel: No matter how simple the matter may be, most of our work is in the proper preparation of the case. And actually in any grievance if the facts were investigated this carefully in the early stages of the grievance procedure you might not have to take as many cases to arbitration. How can you properly handle a dispute unless you've made every effort to find out exactly what happened? We're going to have to analyze thoroughly all the evidence to see whether we should go to arbitration.

Pers. Manager: All right. So far you want a copy of the present agreement and you want a copy of the past agreements and any minutes of the grievance meetings.

COUNSEL: Correct.

PERS. MANAGER: You want to talk to the manager of the store.

COUNSEL: That's correct.

PERS. MANAGER: You want a copy of the report I got from the detective agency and then you want to talk to the person who prepared the report for the detective agency and maybe the shopper who was actually the one who saw her not putting the slips into the packages. Right?

COUNSEL: That's all for the present. And I want that as quickly as possible. The union will probably press for this arbitration to be heard as soon as possible. And don't forget, they might claim retroactive pay. We don't want to let this thing drag on any more than the union does. It could be expensive for us.

PERS. MANAGER: That's right. Is there anything else you want?

COUNSEL: Not for the present. Examining the various documents and interviewing the witnesses may lead to something else I want. If I do want something, whom shall I call upon? You or the store manager?

PERS. MANAGER: You better call on me.

COUNSEL: All right. I don't want to have to work with two or three people. If possible, I'd like to work with one person.

PERS. MANAGER: You better phone me. How fast can we get going on this?

COUNSEL: As soon as we can get all the information. Get me the written material as soon as possible and we can start on that.

PERS. MANAGER: I'll get those to you right away.

COUNSEL: And then I want to talk to Red; the sooner the better.

PERS. MANAGER: I'll take care of that. I'll get going on it right away and if there's anything else, you'll call me.

COUNSEL: All right. Fine. As soon as I have all the necessary information I'll be in a better position to advise you about whether or not we should go to arbitration.

> COMMENT: It will be noted that counsel is seeking to obtain all the information possible on the dispute. Only with this information can he:
>
> 1. determine whether there is a "good case."
>
> 2. begin the preparation of the case for arbitration.
>
> 3. understand the case well enough to develop a preliminary theory of the case, to know whether he will argue the case on a technical theory or whether the case is stronger on an equitable basis, i.e., on a basis of fairness and justice.
>
> Note that counsel repeatedly insisted upon examining all the written documents, in their entirety, before making any judgments concerning the correctness of his client's position on this particular grievance. He was not satisfied to hear about the documents or to see sections of them. He required, for his complete and thorough examination, all written materials which might have any bearing on the case.
>
> Counsel also insisted upon personally interviewing everyone who had any information about the case, including the employer participant in the grievance, the shopper from the Detective Company, and the author of the report of the agency that was submitted to the store.
>
> Only if counsel is given the opportunity to make and does make this thorough preliminary investigation of the case, will he be in a position to intelligently advise whether or not the dispute should go to arbitration, or whether it would be better to settle on the other party's terms. It is often at this crucial point that arbitrations are won or lost. And even more important, if all disputes were thoroughly investigated and considered at

this stage, many cases that should never have gone to arbitration would not have. In fact, if at the negotiation stages of the grievance procedure, the parties had themselves made such a thorough investigation as is suggested here, the case might have been settled by negotiations; without the need to refer it to arbitration.

In addition to getting the facts and deciding how strong a case the party has, there are other factors to consider before deciding whether or not to go to arbitration. Assume that the local union official involved in the clerk case has gone to a higher union official or a union attorney for advice and that they have already reviewed the facts and are going on to other considerations:

Time limits in agreement

COUNSEL: Well, it looks like we have a fairly good case, but before we make any definite move on this, let's talk about a few other points. I notice your agreement provides for certain time limits within which this grievance had to be processed. Were those time limits observed?

UNION: I guess so, nobody has raised any questions about that.

COMMENT: Many grievance procedures contain time limits within which the complaints must be filed, and sometimes even time limits for processing the complaint. Any deviation from time limits or independent agreements changing the time limits should be agreed to in writing by the parties. This will prevent either party later raising the claim that the "statute of limitations" set forth in the agreement has been violated.

COUNSEL: If there are time limits in the agreement, we'd better observe them carefully. Or if we are going to ignore them, we'd better know what we're doing.

UNION: You mean it's better to know you're not

following the agreement than to do it unintentionally.

COUNSEL: Whether you realize it or not, if one party goes over the time limits and the other party does nothing about it, the time limits might not help at all. I remember one case in which this was a crucial issue.

In that case both parties went past the time limits and the union that had filed the complaint didn't claim a default. The parties then agreed to arbitrate. And when the hearing was held the first thing the union did was to ask the arbitrator to rule in its favor because the time limits were not observed. The company claimed that the time limits had been waived or forfeited.

UNION: What did the arbitrator do?

COUNSEL: Here, I'll read part of his opinion on this point:

"Time limits that may be set up in an agreement for the processing of grievances are meant to be observed by the parties as they are specified in the agreement. And when either or both parties continue to operate under the grievance procedure beyond the time limits set forth, it is clear that whatever right they may have had with reference to such time limits they have determined to waive. In this case both the union and the company by their conduct with reference to certain of the grievances did waive any rights they may have had with reference to the application of time limitations."

UNION: I see what you mean. I'll remember that. There's something else I've been wondering about. If we do decide to go to arbitration, how do we get an arbitrator?

Choosing an arbitrator

COUNSEL: Well, there are a number of persons around here who have acted as arbitrators. They have had experience; they have learned the ropes, so to speak, and by their past awards have shown that they are fair men who try to decide cases on the record. The union and employer representatives can usually pick an arbitrator from this group.

UNION: Yes. But suppose you don't have such a group, or you can't agree on someone in the group? Is there any place you can go to get suggestions?

COUNSEL: Yes. There are several sources that can be consulted with respect to obtaining the names of prospective arbitrators. One is the Federal Mediation Service. They give you a panel of arbitrators, if you request it, from which the parties can choose one. Also some State Conciliation Services supply lists. Another source is the American Arbitration Association which provides a similar service.

UNION: Suppose you do have a list of names—how do you decide on the particular person?

COUNSEL: Usually either by mutual agreement or by picking one by lot.

COMMENT: The method of choosing an arbitrator from a submitted list of names varies. The parties may jointly examine such a list and agree upon a selection. They may alternately strike names from the list with the last remaining name receiving the appointment as arbitrator. Or they may put the names in a hat and draw one of them who is then appointed as arbitrator.

UNION: When you are picking an arbitrator how would you decide which is the "best" one?

COUNSEL: It depends a lot on the type of case you may be arbitrating.

UNION: Take this dispute for example. If we can get it to arbitration one issue has to do with interpretation of language in an agreement. So, would you pick a lawyer?

COUNSEL: Not necessarily. Some lawyers may not have any or enough background in every day labor relations. But if they do, then an attorney might be preferable. However, there are non-lawyer arbitrators who can do the job.

The main thing is to get someone who can interpret and apply agreement language in a fair and sensible way.

UNION: The employers suggested a guy who used to represent employers. I'd never take a man like that.

COUNSEL: I don't agree with you. I always like to have a person who has had practical experience in labor relations. I don't care if he got his experience representing employers or unions.

UNION: How could they be impartial?

Ignorance and impartiality

COUNSEL: Don't equate ignorance with impartiality. I'll never forget the case I had in which the employer ruled out individuals by groups. He wouldn't have professors, politicians, judges, lawyers, social workers, government employees, former employer or union representatives.

UNION: Did you get an arbitrator?

COUNSEL: Yes, a retired Rear Admiral of the Navy.

UNION: What happened?

COUNSEL: He gave the union a fine award. The employer made a terrible error. He thought that in order to be fair and impartial the arbitrator had to know absolutely nothing about labor relations, or to have had absolutely no experience in that field. This is, of course, nonsense.

UNION: Do you have to get a different arbitrator for each kind of case?

COUNSEL: No. Some persons have had enough experience as arbitrators in the field of labor relations so that they can qualify for any kind of case.

UNION: Well, what about the dispute we have now. Do you think we can get a good arbitrator for that?

Cost of arbitration

COUNSEL: Oh, yes, I think so. But that does bring up the whole matter of cost of arbitration. One part of the cost of arbitration is the compensation for the arbitrator. Obviously we want an arbitrator that is able, competent, and experienced. Remember, the arbitrator is usually a professional person, a specialist, and must be paid accordingly. You shouldn't go bargain hunting for this kind of service.

Fees of arbitrator

COMMENT: Arbitrators' fees vary. There should be no hesitancy to discuss fees with prospective arbitrators. Ordinarily arbitrators charge a flat fee for hearing time, i.e., so much per hearing day. And an hourly rate for study time. If traveling is involved he will charge for travel expense and travel time.

Parties generally know or can ascertain the range of prevailing rates for arbitrators' fees in their community, and may be able to learn the charges made by a particular arbitrator before contacting him.

UNION: Some of our members think that arbitrations cost too much.

COUNSEL: I know. That's why I'm explaining this to you. If you decide an issue is important enough to arbitrate, then you'd better be prepared to spend some money on it. Sometimes it costs more to leave something unsettled than it costs to get it settled, even if you have to go to arbitration to do it.

UNION: I guess there's the legal fee if we have counsel present our case?

COUNSEL: You're right, that should also be considered as a part of the cost of arbitration. There's also another cost item. And that is the transcript of the hearing. If we want the arbiter to decide the case on the record, we have to give him a record.

UNION: Yes, but that's pretty expensive, isn't it?

COUNSEL: It isn't really as expensive as it seems. After all, if we're going to a lot of trouble and expense to prepare and argue the case, we want to be sure that the arbitrator has all the facts and arguments we presented in a form that he can review at the same time he makes his decision. And that means you should have a reporter to provide a verbatim report of the proceedings, the testimony of the witnesses, so that the arbitrator will have a clear and complete record at the time he decides the case.

COMMENT: There is always much discussion concerning the cost of arbitration. The parties can control this situation.

If they would do a good or even better job at the various negotiating stages of the grievance procedure, they could avoid arbitration and, therefore, its costs.

But obviously some matters must go to arbitration. And as to these items the cost of arbitration is purely a relative matter. The long run cost of leaving a dispute unsettled may be considerably more than the cost of arbitration.

When the parties must resort to arbitration, there are ways of keeping costs down, but not by short cuts or gimmicks that prevent the arbitration process from properly functioning. Nor should costs be cut by sacrificing a full and fair hearing, so that the case is decided on the basis of something less than a complete record.

The best way to cut the costs of arbitration (short of avoiding it completely) is to fully and carefully prepare the case. This will shorten the hearing time and the time required by the arbitrator to study the record. And it is the arbitrator's fee that is one of the larger items in the total cost of arbitration.

The steps in the preparation procedure which are discussed elsewhere in the book that are likely to reduce the cost of arbitration include the following:

1. Thoroughly investigate the grievance. This might lead to settlement.

2. Stipulate to as many facts as possible, thus reducing hearing time.

3. Reduce the number of points in issue by use of pre-hearing meetings.

4. Consider alternative ways of presenting evidence (e.g., exhibits, depositions, even limiting the number of witnesses).

5. Prepare witnesses in advance of the hearings, so that their examination is direct and short.

6. Know your case so thoroughly that you can present it in a rapid, efficient, and orderly manner.

7. Perhaps the case can be presented by briefs. So there would be no need for a formal hearing or transcript.

It must be emphasized that while costs are important, they should be considered secondary to maintaining the integrity of the arbitration process. This means providing a full and fair hearing, and a complete record from which the arbitrator should be required to make his decision. If the dispute is worth taking to litigation, i.e., arbitration, it is worth going "first cabin." Otherwise settle, compromise, or withdraw the complaint.

UNION: Where will the hearing be?

COUNSEL: That's more or less up to us and the employer. We should get a hearing room which will be large enough and comfortable enough so everybody will be reasonably comfortable and so that the arbitrator will have the right facilities. It isn't too hard to find. Hotels have meeting rooms, or some arbitrators have offices large enough to hold their hearings there.

UNION: Okay. Well, listen, I'm going to report all this to the Executive Board and see what they think.

COUNSEL: All right. Let me know as soon as you can what you decide about going to arbitration. If we are going to arbitration, there's a lot more work that has to be done.

CHECKLIST: SHOULD THE DISPUTE GO TO ARBITRATION?

The following is a summary of some of the *pre-arbitration considerations* which should be discussed and weighed before final determination to proceed to arbitration. This process should be pursued by both the employer and the union, with their counsel if they use one, or within their own circles if they do not use an outside counsel.

The checklist includes the following:

1. Examine the agreement, the correspondence, the complaint. In short, thoroughly examine all the written material that might bear on the arbitration proceeding.

2. Obtain as many facts, and not second-hand facts, as possible at this stage of the consideration, at least enough to evaluate your case and develop a preliminary theory of your case.

3. Check time limitations, if any, affecting the various steps in the grievance procedure.

4. Consider the type of arbitrator that might be selected in the specific case in question, and how he might be selected.

5. Consider the relationship between the type of case involved and the arbitrator who might be selected.

6. Decide what kind of a case is involved, solely one of agreement interpretation, or one that could also include equity considerations.

7. Determine the probable cost of the arbitration: the arbitrator's fees, the attorney's or representative's fees, cost of transcript, rental of the hearing room.

8. Consider the effect of winning or of losing the case.

It is the weighing of all these factors, (and the weight will differ in every case), which should determine whether the grievance should proceed beyond the negotiation stage to the terminal point of arbitration itself. There can be many instances where the weight of any one of or a combination of the above factors would lead to a decision to avoid arbitration, even though the moving party believes that it has a "good" case, which could not be settled in the negotiation stages of the grievance procedure.

CHAPTER IV

HOW TO PREPARE THE ARBITRATION CASE

When should you start preparing for arbitration? Clearly, part of the preparation takes place during the preliminary investigation which is required before the parties can decide whether or not to take the case to arbitration. But the real preparation begins even before that. It begins the moment the grievance occurs. The way the first line supervisor and the shop steward or business agent handle the problem is part of the preparation of the case. If all grievances were thoroughly investigated and carefully handled at the very earliest stages, far fewer cases would go to arbitration. In effect, everything that is done or said at any stage of the grievance process becomes a part of the case preparation.

After the preliminary investigation, and after weighing all the pros and cons of taking the case to arbitration, if the parties do decide to go to arbitration, there are additional preparatory steps before presenting the case at the arbitration hearing.

The following conversation between an employer attorney and his assistant will illustrate the various steps involved in the final preparation of the case. The same conversation might take place between union representatives preparing the case. The counsel and his assistant are discussing the grievance of Mrs. Green, which was the subject of the conversations in the previous chapter:

> COUNSEL: You haven't worked on an arbitration case before, have you? We have one in the office now, and this is as good a time as any to get started. I want you to work with me on this case which concerns a clerk at one of our client's stores.
>
> ASSISTANT: All right.
>
> **Identify issues** COUNSEL: It looks now as if this case will involve two issues. Was the clerk discharged, or did she quit;

and is she entitled to sick leave pay for certain days when she was out ill?

Here is a brief statement of facts that I had prepared after interviewing the personnel manager.

I'll tell you what I want you to do. First——

ASSISTANT: Wait just a minute—since this is my first case I wonder if you would go through all the steps you would take to prepare the case. I think I'd learn more that way than just to have you tell me what you want done. If I don't understand what you mean or why you do something, I'll ask questions.

COUNSEL: All right. That's a good idea.

Analyze agreement
Apply agreement to facts

Here's what I do. First I take the agreement and analyze it from all four corners. Generally your client will indicate what he considers the pertinent provisions of the agreement, but quite often there are other related provisions in the agreement that might have been overlooked. So I insist upon analyzing the entire current agreement. In doing that, I work out the relationships between the relevant sections and then see how they apply to the facts in terms of a prima facie case or a prima facie defense. When that's been done, and I'm certain I've identified the provisions of the current agreement, then I take the preceding agreements and compare those provisions to see what changes occurred over the years.

ASSISTANT: How do you do that?

Analyze agreement changes

COUNSEL: Well, for instance, let's take Section 15 of this agreement. Section 15 concerns the right to discharge employees and that will certainly be a crucial section in this case. I want you to trace that section back through all the preceding agreements between the parties. Note any changes of wording that occurred in the section. You might have to hunt for it in each agreement because the section numbers don't always stay the same.

ASSISTANT: I see. I would make a record of all

changes that have been made in that section. In short, you want a history of the provision.

COUNSEL: Yes, but more than that. If no changes occurred, I want to know that too.

If you find changes occurred in the agreement then we're going to have to find out why they occurred. To do this, you'll have to dig for appropriate witnesses and refresh their memories as to just why those changes took place, what happened in negotiations to affect those changes at that particular time, and why the changes were made. And find out, too, if the union made any proposals for changes that it failed to get. That could be valuable information.

That will give us a picture of the development of the agreement terms. Remember, the agreement is the key document. We have to understand how that agreement affects our management rights and which, if any, of our rights it clearly protects.

ASSISTANT: I can certainly see that. I hope the personnel manager has a file of past agreements.

COUNSEL: Probably he does. But if not, you'll have to find out who does. Also see if there have been any past grievances or arbitrations between the parties on the same kind of issues we have in this case. These could be very important to us.

Historical file of agreements

COMMENT: Every employer and union should maintain a continuous history of their collective bargaining agreements. Changes in the agreement and additions or deletions should be documented. Pertinent dates, and reasons for alterations should be noted in writing. An accurately annotated set of agreements will pay important dividends. They will save time in conducting negotiations, and in the handling of grievances and arbitrations. They will make available a clear picture of the development of the provisions.

Parties will, at times, seek to obtain conditions through grievance arbitration which they failed to obtain in negotiations. This should not be permitted. This can usually be prevented if the negotiation history concerning the provision in issue is offered as evidence at the arbitration hearing. Likewise, a good record should be kept of all past grievances and arbitrations.

Counsel: Now about the witnesses——

Assistant: Just a minute, I notice you have some other documents on your desk. Could we go through all the written material first?

Analyze record of grievance meetings

Counsel: I was going to come to those later, but since you raise the point, let's go through them. During the course of these grievance matters there are usually meetings between the parties. I always try to ascertain whether minutes were kept at these meetings. In this particular case the minutes were not jointly approved. These minutes of the meeting were prepared by our client so we look at them with a questioning eye. The union might claim that they are inaccurate. But they do give us a summary of what occurred and how the grievance developed through the grievance procedure.

I want you to analyze those papers carefully from the point of view of the argument that the employer is making. Then check back in the agreements to see if those arguments are supported by the agreements.

And then I want you to analyze those grievance minutes from the point of view of what the union is contending. We will have to anticipate as best we can the union's arguments, the union's point of view, and what it relies upon. That's the only way we can prepare our own affirmative case and our defense against the other side's contentions.

Assistant: Do you plan to make exhibits of any of these minutes?

Counsel: Perhaps. But first I want you to analyze these minutes from the point of view of other factors. Are they helpful to our point of view or are they detrimental to our point of view? If they are helpful, make extra copies. Then if I introduce them as evidence there will be copies for the arbitrator and counsel.

ASSISTANT: Can you introduce such minutes in evidence?

Minutes as evidence

COUNSEL: Not always. But if counsel or one of their witnesses makes some statement referring to them, that would give us an opportunity to try to put them in evidence.

ASSISTANT: Suppose the minutes are against our interest?

COUNSEL: Then we won't put them in. I'll try to keep them out if the other side tries to introduce them.

COMMENT: Minutes, if they are jointly approved and relevant, may be introduced in evidence. But any offers of settlement should be deleted.

No offer of settlement or compromise should be introduced in evidence. To do so would discourage parties from settling matters during negotiating steps of the grievance procedure.

Minutes kept by each party for its own records should not be permitted in evidence. They could be used to refresh recollections of a participant in the meeting.

ASSISTANT: Then about the only exhibits you might have will be these grievance minutes, if you use them, and the agreement.

Use of exhibits

COUNSEL: That's all I can think of right now. But after we develop the case further we might decide on some others. Exhibits can be very persuasive. An imaginative and well thought out exhibit can often be more effective than any other kind of evidence.

Kind of exhibits

COMMENT: Exhibits should be used to make the point clearly and concisely that the party is attempting to put over. There are many different forms that may be used for exhibits. The exhibits may be narrative. Or they may be diagrams, maps, or illustrations. If there is any statistical or financial information it may be presented in the form of charts, bar graphs, or tables. If charts or graphs are used the figures on which the charts are based should be included on the chart or the chart should be accompanied by a table showing the actual figures.

If the exhibit is used to compare or contrast job duties or practice on a particular subject, the information could be set out in parallel columns with appropriate markings to indicate contrasts or similarities. If the duties of a job are being described, the exhibit may consist of forms used in the course of his work by the employee. Examples of such forms are shipping documents, invoices, inventory records, journals, receipts, and orders. The use of the forms themselves is often much more effective than merely referring to or describing them.

More than one exhibit may properly be put into the record on the same point. If several exhibits are needed to make a point then several should be used. For instance, if a financial problem is involved, one exhibit could be a narrative statement summarizing a balance sheet, another exhibit might be the balance sheet itself, and a third exhibit could be a chart or diagram presentation of certain details contained in the balance sheet.

Source of exhibit

If the exhibit is not the original source of the information, but is computed or constructed from some other source, it should always clearly show the source from which it was derived. And, it is extremely important that the computation or compilation be accurately made. If the other side is able to show errors in the exhibit, it may shake the confidence of the arbitrator in the entire case of the party submitting the faulty exhibit. The exhibit should not contain material quoted out of context. It should not be so constructed that the other side could bring in other material from the same source which could change or substantially modify what the party offering the exhibit sought to show.

Exhibits should be so clear, so simple and uninvolved, that they can be presented without lengthy explanation.

Witnesses: interviewing them

COUNSEL: Let's take up the matter of interviewing the witnesses. I want you to make a written record of those interviews. As I told you, the personnel manager came to see me. His story of what happened was hearsay. The actual person who was involved in this grievance was the store manager. We are going to interview him. He's coming into the office tomorrow. I want you to handle that interview.

ASSISTANT: What do you want me to cover in the interview?

COUNSEL: I want you to sit down with him and get from him exactly what happened from the time the clerk came to work to the time she left the store. I want you to know in detail exactly what happened, how it happened, what was said, when, and by whom. Don't assume we know anything at all about the case. Get every bit of information from him that you can.

ASSISTANT: You want me to make notes of that interview?

COUNSEL: Yes, I want you to make detailed notes. When you interview Red, remember that his conversation with Mrs. Green, the clerk, is very important. We want to know whether she quit or was discharged. We'll have to try and get Red's exact language. A large part of the case may depend on what he said. I want you to do one other thing and I will do it too. Size up the manager as he is telling his story.

ASSISTANT: What do you mean, size him up?

COUNSEL: Try to determine what kind of witness he will make. Does he look honest? Does he handle himself well? Does he answer questions frankly? In short, let me put it this way: Does he impress you with his testimony?

Witnesses: evaluating them

ASSISTANT: I see. I hear he's called Red because he's redheaded. Is he excitable?

COUNSEL: I want you to test that. Ask him a couple of questions which might get him a little mad. Try to antagonize him and see how he handles himself. In fact, get rough with him. Use your toughest cross-examination technique. We want to know what to expect from him as a witness. We have to anticipate that from the union counsel.

If Red is an excellent witness, the union representative may want to prod or needle him to get him to change his story or show that he's a man who would flare up on occasion. This could give substance to the contention that the girl was discharged.

Witnesses: preparing them

ASSISTANT: Let's say we decide to use the witness. Shall we prepare him for the hearing?

COUNSEL: Oh, yes. If we do decide to use him we would certainly want to spend some time preparing him for the hearing. There's nothing wrong, legally or morally, in our determining what the witness will testify to. Unless we do this we have no basis for deciding whether to call him as a witness or not. In fact, unless we do that, we won't know what questions to ask him. That's true of any witnesses we might want to use. Of course, this doesn't mean coaching or telling the witness what to say. That would be legally and morally wrong. After we question the witness and decide that we want to use him, we should put in writing the questions we intend to ask the witness. By that time we should know what to expect as answers. The witness should be pretty familiar with the ground we will cover in the direct examination. If we can figure out what questions the opposing party is likely to ask on cross-examination, we might let the witness know what to expect. We certainly want him to tell the truth. But we want to avoid the kind of surprise question that might throw him into confusion.

COMMENT: Witnesses should be instructed to answer all questions in a concise and straight-forward manner. They should be told only to answer the questions asked of them—they must avoid volunteering information not required by the question. And they should be warned not to get into arguments with their cross-examiner.

Sometimes counsel will ask a witness during cross-examination if he discussed his testimony with anyone. Many laymen have a mistaken notion that such a discussion is not proper. They freeze up, or hesitate, and often reply that they did not have such a discussion, when it is clear that their counsel must have talked to them in order to know what questions to ask on direct examination. The witness's guilty attitude, when in fact he is not guilty of any misconduct, may partially destroy his credibility as a witness. He should be told to reply to any such question in the affirmative.

ASSISTANT: Do you think there will be any other possible witnesses to interview besides Red?

COUNSEL: Yes. There is a detective agency report involved in this case. Apparently our client has a detective agency that sends shoppers around—to see that sales are properly rung up, whether there is any improper handling of cash, and matters like that.

There was a shopper who went to the store and reported that this clerk did not give the customers sales slips. Now, the personnel manager didn't mention it, but I know in one of our former cases there was a store rule with respect to the handling and wrapping of sales. If I remember correctly, that rule provided that at the time of any sale the customer must be given the sales slip and each sale must be rung up.

Company rules   ASSISTANT: Where was this rule? Do we have a copy?

COUNSEL: No, we don't. We're not sure if Mrs. Green has seen a copy of these rules, or whether they were properly posted. The personnel manager didn't raise the point. This sort of thing often happens.

Employers might not mention things like this because they think they are immaterial. But they might be very material and important. Certainly in this case we want a copy of the store rules.

ASSISTANT: Where do I get that?

COUNSEL: From the manager of the store.

ASSISTANT: Is it in writing?

COUNSEL: I assume it is. Be sure you have the copy of the rules in effect at the time of the incident. We don't want to start using the rules and then find out that they aren't the right ones.

ASSISTANT: All right. I'll make a note of that.

COUNSEL: I want you to ask Red exactly how the store rules were handled, where they were posted, were they readable, were they available for inspection by the employees, and particularly by this employee. I also want you to find out under what authority they were issued and posted, or was there anything in the agreement that prohibited them from being posted.

ASSISTANT: You said something about the rules being "readable". What do you mean?

COUNSEL: I had a case where the company claimed they discharged a machinist for violation of a company rule. The rules had been posted. It looked like the company had a cinch case. But the union proved that the machinist did not know the rule. And the arbitrator decided in favor of the union.

ASSISTANT: But I thought you said the rules were posted?

COUNSEL: Yes, but the copy posted was in small type—it had been dittoed and had faded. It would not have been reasonable to expect anyone to know that these were house rules, or to be able to read them if they did know there were such rules. It always seemed to me that if house rules were important enough to be issued, they should be printed in large legible type on cardboard cards no less than 12″ by 14″, and then placed in a number of strategic locations in the plant.

ASSISTANT: You'd think employers would want to make them easy to find and read.

COUNSEL: In some plants it might be a good idea to post copies of the rules translated into other languages where the makeup of the work force makes this advisable. The main point is to communicate the house rules to all employees who might be adversely affected if they should violate them. You can't justify punishing employees for breaking a rule which they didn't know existed.

ASSISTANT: What about the detective agency? What do you want me to do about that?

COUNSEL: Apparently it was a shopper from the detective agency that reported that this clerk did not give him a sales slip. We may have to use this shopper as one of our witnesses, and he should be interviewed as soon as possible.

ASSISTANT: What do you want me to get from him?

COUNSEL: I want you to find out exactly what happened from the time he entered the store to the time he left. Get his complete story.

Cross-examine him just the way you will Red. You will probably find that he made a written memorandum of what occurred. The report, as I understand it, is a typed report probably prepared in the detective agency's office from his notes. I want you to be able to trace what happened in the store; follow it through to his memorandum to the agency and then to the final report that came to the store manager from the agency.

If the final report was prepared by the head of the detective agency then I want you to interview him as to how he prepared the final report, and his basis for it. The report is what we are relying upon, not the shopper's notes.

ASSISTANT: Why is all of this work necessary? You're not going to use all these witnesses, are you?

COUNSEL: It is impossible to be overprepared. The

greater the preparation the better position we're in to put on a good case and defend against the other side and it helps us analyze our own weaknesses and prepare defenses for them.

Personnel file

Now, one other thing I want you to get from the store manager is this clerk's personnel record. That starts from the date of her employment with the store chain. I want you to analyze that record carefully, and I want it in our office so that I can analyze it, too. We want to find out just what type of person we're dealing with. And we want to know as much as we can about her record with the company.

ASSISTANT: All right. Now, what about the sick leave pay complaint. Is there anything special to do on that?

Type of dispute

COUNSEL: Be sure to remember that issue when you're analyzing the agreement and checking for changes in preceding agreements. That looks like what we call a straight "agreement interpretation" problem.

ASSISTANT: Aren't they both agreement interpretation issues?

COUNSEL: In a sense, yes. But in the discharge issue there appears to be a dispute on the facts—what were the clerk's actions, what did she mean by her actions, and then how does the agreement apply to the facts. In the sick pay issue, on the other hand, I think we will find that we all agree on the facts, but we don't agree on the application of the agreement to the facts. We are in dispute on how our agreement affects a particular case even though we agree on the description of the case itself.

ASSISTANT: I see the difference.

Investigate setting of dispute

COUNSEL: There is one other investigation we should make. If the clerk quit or whatever happened, it took place in the back room of the store, in the store manager's office, I think. We should view the premises.

ASSISTANT: Do you want me to go to the store and take a look at the store and the back room?

COUNSEL: Yes, before you interview the witnesses. I want you to go to the store and see the physical set-up. I will probably go with you. I want to see it, too.

ASSISTANT: Do you usually make such visits?

COUNSEL: Yes, always, because it's invaluable in preparing and examining witnesses. I can visualize all the testimony more clearly.

ASSISTANT: Do you think it might be of some help to draw a diagram that maybe you would want to use in the case, showing the location of the door and the checkstand and the back room?

COUNSEL: I'd like to have that very much. We are going to have to illustrate the physical setup of this store and explain what occurred, where the clerk went, how she walked out. It may be very helpful in presenting the case to the arbitrator. The arbitrator may want to see the store but if not, we want to illustrate and explain to the arbitrator where the various incidents occurred.

COMMENT: Where reference is made to the scene of an incident pertinent to the case, diagrams or photographs of such areas should be made available in the hearing. It is far easier to understand the evidence with the aid of such diagrams or photographs. It may be desirable to have the arbitrator actually visit the areas in question.

In cases where it is necessary to describe operations or machines, it is best to have the arbitrator view such operations or machines. Viewing the operations or machines should precede any testimony that may be offered relative to the operations or machines. The arbitrator can then more easily follow the testimony, particularly if it is technical in nature.

ASSISTANT: What's going to be our theory of the 'discharge-quit' issue?

Theory of case   Counsel: There are still a few holes in our facts, but I think we can develop a theory of our case. For instance, we must check the information very carefully to find out if she ever said to the store manager, "I quit." If she did, we're in a pretty good position. If she didn't, then we have to know exactly what she did say when she left the store in a huff. I think we may find that an atmosphere developed during the discussion that made it reasonable for Red, the store manager, to assume that when the clerk picked up her coat and walked out she *was* quitting. If Red assumed she quit, we want to present fully the reasonable basis for that assumption.

Assistant: What if we can't persuade the arbitrator that Red was reasonable in assuming that she quit?

Counsel: We're going to develop sort of a double shot approach. First, we will argue that she quit, or acted in such a way as to lead Red to reasonably believe she quit. But we'll also argue that if she didn't quit she was properly discharged. I think we'll find that Red's statements on the day after the argument could be interpreted as a discharge. This part of the case will be built around the detective agency report and the store rules. We'll assert that by failing to observe the store rule requiring the clerk to give the shopper a register slip, there was proper cause for discharge.

In any case we are going to be limited by the reasons that the employer used as a basis for discharge at the time of discharge. We can't support our claim with any reasons Red might have thought up later.

Assistant: So our theory of the case will be that the clerk quit, but that if she didn't quit she should be considered as having been discharged for proper cause because of her failure to comply with store rules.

Other arbitration   Counsel: Right. We should also take one other
awards   step. I want you to search for arbitration awards

covering similar factual situations. Find out how other arbitrators have ruled. You may not find exactly similar facts, but if they're close enough to raise the same issues study them carefully. Those awards may not influence the arbitrator, but at least they might give us some theories, some arguments, and some ideas that have been used in other cases.

ASSISTANT: Even if we find some favorable rulings, they would never convince the union that we're right on the dispute.

COUNSEL: Don't forget that we're not trying to convince the union. We have a judge up in front of us at the hearing; the arbitrator is our judge. He's the one we have to convince. Remember, the arbitrator is the key man and we should keep him in mind every minute while we're preparing the case. It's true that the awards are not binding on the arbitrator. But they might help to persuade him that either or both of our theories of the case are not out of line, and should be adopted by him.

CHECKLIST: PREPARATION OF THE CASE.

The conversation between the counsel and his assistant illustrates the steps which must be taken to adequately prepare an arbitration case. The steps include:

1. *Analyze the present agreement:* This involves ascertaining the pertinent provisions relating to the dispute, studying the agreement as a whole, and applying the provision to the facts in question.

2. *Study preceding agreements:* The history of the pertinent provisions should be studied to see whether or not any changes have been made. There is an advantage, too, in making such a study for the purpose of discovering other cases that have either been settled under the specific provisions of the agreement by the parties themselves or cases that have gone to arbitration.

3. *Study the grievance committee minutes and other documents presented or used by the grievance committee:* Such a study can be extremely profitable. It will disclose the respective

positions of the parties. It may actually disclose the theory of the case upon which the other party is relying. In any case it gives to an outsider, such as the counsel, or anyone else presenting the case, the background of the dispute.

This background is invaluable in presenting the arbitration case. It is quite clear that the more familiar an advocate becomes with his case, the more intelligently he can present it.

4. *Interview witnesses and make a detailed written record of the interview:* This interview should be distinguished from the direct examination that is conducted at the hearing if the witness is used. The detailed interview is primarily for the information of the counsel. Based upon the interview, counsel will determine (a) whether to use the individual as a witness, and (b) what the nature of his or her direct testimony will be. It is a good practice if counsel determines to use the individual as a witness, to set forth in broad outline the general questions which counsel intends to put to witness upon direct examination. Interviewing a witness is not only useful to obtain the facts, but also to size up the witness, to try to evaluate what kind of an impression the witness will make upon the arbitrator. Is he a witness who will transfer his testimony and evidence with sincerity to the arbitrator? Is he a witness who will stand up under cross-examination, or, even though telling the truth, is he liable to 'blow his top,' so that the overall impression of the witness' good testimony will be lost?

5. *Secure any pertinent documents:* In this particular case, this means getting the store rules; studying them; ascertaining their history; finding out when and where they were posted; whether they were "readable"; finding out whether the store rules have any relationship to the written collective bargaining agreement. As will be noted in a moment, the special emphasis on store rules becomes important since counsel has determined that it will play an important role in his affirmative theory of the case.

6. *Intensively study the claimant's personnel record:* This allows counsel to become familiar with anything that the personnel record may disclose about the employee's character, work record, personality and other information concerning her.

7. *Visit and view the scene of the dispute:* This preparation

can be of great value to counsel. As counsel pointed out to his assistant, he is better able to visualize the testimony if he can see where the events were supposed to have occurred. And in so doing, he may be more successful in transmitting to the arbitrator his particular point of view in his presentation of the arbitration case. A diagram may prove very helpful. In many cases, such diagrams or even photographs should be introduced at the arbitration proceeding so that the arbitrator will be aided in visualizing the actual scene of the dispute. And, of course, as is done in many cases, it might be valuable to have the arbitrator visit the scene of the dispute if such a visitation will aid in presenting the case to him.

8. *Prepare the witnesses:* The parties should decide what witnesses will be used at the hearing. These witnesses should be prepared by going over the subject matter and by being told what questions will be asked in direct examination, and what questions they might expect in cross-examination.

9. *Decide upon and prepare the exhibits:* Exhibits form an important part of the record. They should be approached imaginatively with due recognition of their persuasive value. And they should be prepared thoughtfully and carefully.

10. *Develop the theory of the case:* It will be noted that counsel expects to be able to develop a theory of the case from this detailed preparation. He has already done so on a preliminary basis from his preliminary investigation. But now he has to make a final determination of how he intends to proceed. He must decide his theory so that all the evidence will be pointed toward supporting his theory and all the evidence he can get in his favor will constitute a defense of the theory of the other side. Therefore, he must not only develop a theory of his own case, but attempt to ascertain the theory of the opposition.

In this particular arbitration, it is quite clear what the opposition theory will be. Namely, that the employee was discharged and did not quit; the employer's theory is that she quit and was not discharged.

And in order to bolster the theory that Mrs. Green quit, the employer will seek to rely upon the fact that she quit because she walked off the job. Then the employer will develop what can be called a secondary theory: That if the arbitrators accept the position that she did not quit, that then she was discharged for proper cause; that cause being violation of store rules by failing to put the cash register tapes in the packages. And this latter theory rests on the store rules, their alleged violation, and the evidence supplied to the store by the Detective Company.

CHAPTER V

THE SUBMISSION AGREEMENT

A submission agreement sets forth the specific issue to be arbitrated. It may also contain procedural details governing the arbitration. The drafting of a complete and proper submission agreement is of primary importance. The statement of the issue may be negotiated between the parties or may appear on the written grievance. The better practice would be to formulate a submission agreement for each grievance, and not use the written grievance as it was first filed.

The suggestion that a complete submission agreement be drafted may seem too formal in its approach. But observing this suggestion would require the parties to meet together and negotiate the terms of such an agreement. Such a negotiation may lead to a settlement without the need of going to arbitration. This can result when the parties seek to define and agree upon the specific issue to be arbitrated. They may find that they are not too far apart for a negotiated settlement. In short, it provides another opportunity to settle the dispute without going to arbitration. This prophylactic result that may flow from negotiating the submission agreement is of great importance.

Additionally, by formally negotiating the agreement, the parties can sharpen the issues they desire to arbitrate. And the authority of the arbitrator is thus more specifically defined. Finally, much time can be saved at the hearings if the preliminary work involved in drafting a submission agreement is done prior to the arbitration hearings.

The following discussion illustrates a simple negotiation of a submission agreement for the case involving Mrs. Green. The union representative and employer representative are meeting together prior to the arbitration to draft the submission agreement.

UNION: Well, it looks like we have an arbitration case on Ann Green. I still think you should put her back to work. It isn't too late to forget about arbitrating it.

COMMENT: At every stage of preparations for arbitration, both parties should remember that efforts to settle the matter by negotiation should continue. Sometimes the realization that the case is set for arbitration itself helps to create a more favorable atmosphere for such a settlement.

EMPLOYER: I wish we could settle it. But we are convinced Mrs. Green quit. We have already replaced her, so it would mean firing her replacement. Besides, this other question she raises on sick leave should be settled, too. It could easily come up again.

Contents of submission agreement

UNION: We'd better work out a submission agreement then so that we know exactly what we're asking the arbitrator to decide. We don't have any problem about the arbitrator; we've already agreed on him. We should put that in our submission agreement though, shouldn't we?

EMPLOYER: Yes, I think we should.

There is one other point with respect to his appointment. You know the agreement provides that there shall be a board of three arbitrators, one appointed by the union, one appointed by the employer, and one appointed by both. I don't think we need a three-man board in this case, do you?

UNION: No, I don't know why we would. Why don't we include in the submission agreement that we stipulate that the decision of the single arbitrator shall be final and binding and that the provisions of the contract as to a board of arbitration are waived?

EMPLOYER: That's a good idea. I know you wouldn't do it, but somebody might get the bright idea we didn't follow the agreement procedures and claim that the award was void. I agree we ought to cover those items in the submission agreement.

Single arbitration v. board of arbitration

COMMENT: There are conflicting views as to whether the case should be submitted to a single arbitrator or to a so-called board of arbitration, consisting of an equal number of representatives of the employer and the union, with the chairman of the board of arbitration being the neutral selected by both parties.

It is suggested that in most, if not all instances, the so-called board of arbitration adds very little to the efficiency of the arbitration proceeding. The fact remains that the persons sitting with the neutral arbitrator are actually advocates. They represent the parties themselves. They should be called party-arbitrators. Therefore, in most instances, they do not add a neutral or impartial point of view to the proceedings. It is true that in a few cases these party-arbitrators approach the issues as impartial arbitrators and vote accordingly.

It has been argued that party-arbitrators may aid the arbitrator in his consideration of the record, particularly with reference to technical matters that may be involved in the dispute. The counter-suggestion is that such aid can be given at the hearings. The arbitrator has the authority to call the parties back into session if he needs some technical aid. In most instances the so-called "technical aid" is an attempt by argument or even evidence which is not in the record to persuade the arbitrator to rule in favor of one party or the other.

What usually happens when there is a board is that the party-arbitrators attempt to bargain with the arbitrator for the decision. And this results in little, if any, weight being given to the actual record of evidence which was produced at the hearing. If the arbitrator permits himself to be used in such a fashion, the whole point of an arbitration proceeding is lost; namely, that a decision will be made based upon the record. If the parties desire to negotiate or compromise then they are certainly free to do so. But the arbitration process itself should not be used as a vehicle for negotiation after the case has been submitted for decision.

The arbitration process is a form of private judicial determination which has been adapted by long experience to aid in settling labor-management disputes. It should be preserved for that end, and decisions resulting from arbitration should be grounded upon evidence presented at the hearing; not upon either argument or evidence brought forth for the first time in executive session of the board of arbitration. Nor should the arbitrator be placed in the position where, in effect, he has to bargain with one or the other party-arbitrators to obtain his vote in order to arrive at a majority decision.

UNION: Now, let's consider the cost of the arbitration. We ought to provide that the cost should be divided equally between the two parties.

Cost of arbitration

EMPLOYER: By cost, you mean the cost of the reporter and the arbitrator, and that each side will pay its own cost, including attorney's fees?

UNION: That's right. Suppose we do it that way even if we don't put it in writing, but maybe we should cover it.

EMPLOYER: Yes. We certainly should cover the cost in the agreement. We can say: "Each side will bear one-half of the cost of the arbitrator and the reporter and such other costs incurred at the direction of the arbitrator."

UNION: That's a good way to put it. That would, of course, include the cost of the hearing room we're going to rent and similar items.

EMPLOYER: That's correct.

UNION: All right. We'll put that in.

We should also provide that the decision of the arbitrator will be final and binding on both parties.

EMPLOYER: I always include that. Under our state law, the award would be binding anyway, but, if you put it right in the submission agreement, if there is any argument about it, we can say, "There it is in black and white; that's what we agreed."

Award: final and binding

UNION: I had an interesting experience on that. I was called over to another state by one of my clients to advise them on an arbitration they had pending in that state. I found out by a little research that arbitration awards were not specifically enforceable in that state. Under that kind of a law, a party can withdraw from an arbitration at any time up to the award and the other party that prevails might have some difficulty in enforcing it. In that kind of a situation obviously this final and binding provision of our submission agreement is essential. In this day and age when communication and travel is so easy across state lines, we do have to be careful about that.

EMPLOYER: Along that same line we might consider adding a clause that when arbitration proceedings start, we submit ourselves to the jurisdiction of the arbitrator and empower him to render a final and binding award, regardless of whether one party leaves or not. That is, we agree to a default award.

UNION: Yes. I agree to that.

COMMENT: To provide that the award is "final and binding" does not necessarily mean that the parties have waived such legal rights as they may have under appropriate law. (See Appendix C.) A party may, under certain circumstances, go to court for the purposes of modifying or correcting an award, or to have an award vacated. If the court finds that the arbitrator has exceeded his jurisdiction the award will be vacated. This would also be true in case of a default award.

Now, there is one other provision in the submission agreement that I sometimes think is helpful. We have a grievance arbitration here where we are proceeding under the terms of an agreement. While I think this arbitrator understands his authority, it has happened that, in my experience, arbitrators have gone beyond the terms of the agreement and in effect by their award amended the collective bargaining agreement.

Arbitrator: limitations on

I assume neither of us wants that to happen. Perhaps we can put in a clause that will make it clear he doesn't have the right to amend or add to or subtract from any of the provisions of the agreement.

EMPLOYER: That's fine. I think the arbitrator we have selected would know that limitation very well and, of course, the agreement will be in evidence. But let's make it specific, that he has no authority to amend, alter, or change any of the provisions of the agreement itself. We can state exactly that in the submission agreement.

Procedural rules

UNION: All right. We'll do that.

What about procedural rules? Do we want to state any rules in the agreement?

EMPLOYER: I doubt that it's necessary in this case. We've used this arbitrator before and we know how he operates. He always allows a full and fair hearing and the right to examine and cross-examine witnesses.

UNION: Well, let's put in such a provision anyway.

COMMENT: If the arbitration is under the auspices of a particular association, many rules can be incorporated by reference. For example, if parties are arbitrating by agreement in accordance with the American Arbitration Association Rules, then such rules are considered incorporated in the submission agreement by merely referring to them. If this is done, the parties should carefully read the rules before agreeing to them. Some of the rules may be changed or made inapplicable by agreement between the parties.

Issue to be submitted

EMPLOYER: Now, we'd better get down to one of the important items, the issue, the question to be submitted to the arbitrator. We want to clearly define his authority.

And I guess we've all found that too little time is spent on the wording of the precise question. With that in mind, I have worked very carefully on a question that I think is entirely fair. May I submit this to you as the question we will present to the arbitrator?

UNION: Yes, surely.

EMPLOYER: (1) "Was Mrs. Green justified in quitting her employment on July 10, 1959?" (2) "Was Mrs. Green absent because of illness for four working days during May, 1958?"

UNION: I appreciate the care with which you have considered these questions. But I hope you didn't expect to win the arbitration before it even starts by the form of the question you propose. The basic issue here, so far as the union is concerned, is that the clerk didn't quit at all. Rather, we claim that she was discharged improperly under the terms of the agreement. So you're asking me by your proposed question to admit in advance that she quit. I couldn't accept that kind of a question. And then on the sick leave question. We're not claiming Mrs. Green was absent four working days. We can't prove that. Further, nobody ever raised the question that she was actually sick.

EMPLOYER: I see what you mean. First, on the question whether the clerk quit or was discharged— would you agree with a statement such as this: Did Mrs. Green quit or was she discharged? That's what we want the arbitrator to decide, isn't it?

UNION: Not quite. He could decide that she was discharged but we still wouldn't know whether we could insist on your putting her back to work. We're claiming she was discharged in violation of the terms of the agreement.

EMPLOYER: Well, of course, our position goes further, too. We claim that if she was discharged, she was discharged properly for violation of store rules.

UNION: I know you're going to argue that.

There are two ways, as you know, that we can set up the issues in the submission agreement. We can set forth the respective contentions of the parties, as we have been discussing here, and ask the arbitrator to determine which contention is correct, and that would be his award, or we can ask him a question to which, in effect, he could answer "yes" or "no".

Probably either procedure would work in this case. Let's try this one: "Did Mrs. Green quit her employment with the Z Company or was she discharged in violation of the terms of the agreement?" If the arbitrator rules that Mrs. Green was discharged in violation of the agreement, the union requests that she be reinstated with full rights as to seniority and back pay from the last date of her employment." That is the question we want answered and it permits each of us to present our respective contentions.

EMPLOYER: That seems like a fair statement.

UNION: All right. Now let's consider the sick leave question. As I said before, we're not claiming that Mrs. Green was absent for four working days because of illness. We're arguing that the sick leave clause in the agreement doesn't require that the minimum of three days be working days. It just says "days" and we think that means calendar days. She was sick four calendar days.

EMPLOYER: I don't see how she can claim anything if you don't argue she was out for at least three working days. Nobody would think the agreement means anything else.

UNION: Well, we think the provision means calendar days and we're going to argue that to the arbitrator. And we want the statement of the issue broad enough so that we can argue that way. Why don't we just state it, "Is Mrs. Green entitled to sick leave pay?"

EMPLOYER: That's not specific enough. We should include the exact dates which we are arguing about. After all, this isn't an abstract question. In this case, we're really asking the arbitrator to decide how to interpret the agreement provision. Maybe we should state the specific issue which can be answered with a "yes" or "no" and then also include the issue: What shall be the application of Article 12 of the Agreement dated April 1, 1958, as this paragraph pertains to the "three day period?" Shall the application be "calendar days" as contended by the union, or "scheduled work days of the employee" as contended by the company? That way, we'll have the question completely settled.

Reduce agreement to writing

UNION: That's all right with me. Well, I think we understand each other on the issues. From my notes, let me dictate the agreement right now to my secretary while you are here.

> COMMENT: Ordinarily some of the items that should be placed in the submission agreement may already appear in the collective bargaining agreement provision dealing with arbitration. In such cases those items can be covered by incorporating the collective bargaining provision by reference, and then adding any new items or conditions necessary for this particular dispute. Or the submission agreement can restate what already appears in the collective bargaining agreement provision along with the additional items. The agreement herein dictated is of the latter type.

UNION: Miss Steno, please take the following, and type three copies.

Arbitration Submission Agreement. This agreement, made this tenth day of July, _____, by and between the Z Company and the X Union.

1. The parties to this agreement are signators to a collective bargaining agreement dated April 1, 1960. Section 20 of that agreement provides for the settlement of grievances by a Board of Arbitrators.

2. The Company and the Union have not been able to reach a settlement on union grievance No. 221, involving Mrs. Ann Green, clerk at the Z store.

Therefore, in accordance with the terms of Section 20, the grievance is hereby submitted for arbitration.

3. The Company and Union hereby waive the provisions of Section 20 which provide for a three-man Board of Arbitration, and have agreed that Mr. A. shall be the sole arbitrator in this matter.

4. The Employer and the Union agree to accept the decision of the arbitrator as final and binding. The arbitrator is empowered to render a final and binding award even if one party defaults, that is, fails to put in an appearance at the hearing.

5. Each party will pay one-half of the cost of the fee of the arbitrator, and the costs incurred at the direction of the arbitrator, including other costs of the arbitrator's copy of the transcript.

6. The arbitrator has no authority to amend, alter, or change any of the provisions of the agreement between the Z Company and the X Union.

7. The place, date, and time for the hearing shall be set by the arbitrator to meet the mutual convenience of the parties and the arbitrator.

8. Each of the parties shall be given a full and fair hearing. The right to examine and cross-examine witnesses shall be accorded both parties.

9. The arbitrator shall state the effective date of his award, including the effective date of retroactive pay, if any, granted to Mrs. Green.

10. The specific issues submitted for arbitration are as follows:

A. Did Mrs. Green quit her employment with the Z Company, or was she discharged in violation of the terms of the agreement?

If the arbitrator rules that Mrs. Green was discharged in violation of the terms of the agreement, the Union requests reinstatement with full rights as to seniority and back pay from the last date of Mrs. Green's employment.

B. (1) Is Mrs. Green entitled to sick leave pay for May 1 and May 4?

(2) What shall be the application of Article 12 of the agreement dated April 1, 1960, as this paragraph pertains to the "three-day period?" Shall the application be "calendar days" as contended by the Union or "scheduled work days" as contended by the Company?

UNION: Miss Steno, please provide the usual lines for signatures. Thank you.

Chapter VI

ARRANGING FOR THE ARBITRATION

The process of arranging for an arbitration includes a number of housekeeping details which are important and should not be overlooked by anyone who is preparing for an arbitration hearing.

The following telephone conversation between an arbitrator and counsel will illustrate some of the housekeeping matters involved in an arbitration:

COUNSEL: As you know, I represent the X Union.

ARBITRATOR: Yes.

Notifying arbitrator of his appointment
COUNSEL: The union has a dispute with the Z Company which is now going to arbitration. The attorney for the employer and I adopted the procedure of exchanging a list of arbitrators, five from each, and your name appeared on both lists. As a result of that we have agreed mutually on you as the arbitrator for this case.

Employer's counsel has asked me to call you to tell you of your appointment and to discuss the procedure for the hearing.

ARBITRATOR: Thank you very much. Just for my records, after our conversation I'd appreciate a letter from both you and the Employer's counsel noting my appointment. Have you agreed to a submission agreement?

COUNSEL: Yes. We'll send it along with your notice of appointment.

ARBITRATOR: What about pre-hearing briefs?

COUNSEL: We prefer not to file any.

66

COMMENT: Sometimes the parties want to file pre-hearing briefs. These are actually written opening statements. If the parties have stipulated to some facts they include these in the briefs. In practice, when pre-hearing briefs are filed, the parties nevertheless cover much of the same ground in their oral presentation.

ARBITRATOR: Where are you going to have the hearing?

COUNSEL: We haven't done anything about that. What's your suggestion?

Hearing room

ARBITRATOR: Well, the last time I was in an arbitration (not with you, gentlemen), we had a room that was very bad for a hearing. The light wasn't good, the ventilation was bad, and it filled up with smoke very rapidly.

Please get a room that is well lighted and well ventilated. People get pretty tired as the hearing progresses and if the physical surroundings aren't reasonably comfortable, they become irritable and many times we have arguments in the arbitration hearing we ought not to have.

Then, make arrangements for drinking water and glasses, and some writing pads and pencils.

Arrange enough legible copies of exhibits

Then there is one other thing, and again I'm just pointing this out as a matter of form, as I do whenever I'm selected, if there are going to be exhibits in the case—and I assume there will be, won't there?

COUNSEL: I believe there probably will be.

ARBITRATOR: Can you make it a point, and also ask counsel for the other party to have enough copies of exhibits so that I will get a copy and the reporter will get a copy (and I want to talk about that in a moment), and each counsel will have a copy. And the copies should be readable. I've had some copies that were so badly duplicated that nobody could have read them.

COUNSEL: We'll be sure to take care of that.

COMMENT: If counsel knows he is going to use a large number of exhibits, he should prepare them punched for loose leaf ring hard cover binders. Binders should be supplied to the arbitrator, opposition counsel, and to the reporter. This provides a neat and orderly method of preserving the exhibits as they are presented. It adds a precision to the presentation of the case and assures that the arbitrator will have all of the exhibits in one place, making them readily available and easy to work with.

Use of a reporter

ARBITRATOR: Have you discussed employing a reporter?

COUNSEL: Well, I know from past cases, you always like to have a reporter. However, I don't like to tell you this, but in this particular case my client hasn't had many of these arbitrations, and they do not want a reporter. They are trying to save money. I'm having a little difficulty getting over to them the real need for a reporter. Maybe you can help me on that.

ARBITRATOR: I assume they want this case decided on what you and I would call the record?

COUNSEL: That's correct.

ARBITRATOR: All right. Now, I think you ought to point out to them and make it clear that there are only two ways to have a complete record of the case: Either the matter is submitted completely on briefs, and you gentlemen can do that if you want to, or if we are going to have hearings, then there should be a transcript of the entire proceeding.

Tell them that if they expect me to sit at the hearing and make notes, I won't have a chance to listen too closely to the testimony. I'm no shorthand reporter and I can't make notes of everything that's said. And as you know, something might be said in the afternoon of a day's hearing that is important only if I know what was said in the morning of the hearing, and that may be the one item that I did not record in my notes.

COUNSEL: That's a good point.

ARBITRATOR: You see what I mean. If I'm taking it down in longhand, how would I know what to select to take down, until after I've heard the whole case? So, you tell them that as a matter of practice I prefer them to have a reporter, but if they think it's too expensive, let them submit the whole matter on briefs. Of course, there may be instances in which the case could be heard without a reporter, particularly where witnesses are not used. But the better practice is to use a reporter.

The advocates, in a case without other witnesses, may themselves testify to certain matters within their knowledge. This fact, in addition to the fact that the oral arguments of the advocates should be a part of the record, makes a reporter desirable.

COUNSEL: Thanks. I think we can work this out.

ARBITRATOR: There's still another advantage to a transcript: The existence of a written record— a transcript or briefs—is a very important incentive to make arbitrators stay with the record when they come to write their opinion and decision.

COUNSEL: That is an important use of the transcript.

ARBITRATOR: And the transcript is insurance for the arbitrator—if some party claims that certain matters were not placed in evidence—or if they question some of the testimony.

COMMENT: It should be noted that some parties object to the use of reporters in arbitration hearings. Reasons advanced against their use include cost, and the feeling that a reporter makes a hearing too formal or legalistic. Some arbitrators share these views.

Another view suggests using reporters only in the "most complicated and lengthy cases."

COUNSEL: What about the time for the hearing?

Date of hearing   ARBITRATOR: Submit two or three dates to me and we will pick out a mutually agreeable one for the hearing.

COUNSEL: All right. We are anxious that this matter proceed quickly.

ARBITRATOR: Well, I think I can accommodate myself to the parties' desire to move rapidly on this case.

CHECKLIST: ARRANGING THE HEARING

As mentioned in the foregoing conversation, the housekeeping arrangements for an arbitration include the following:

1. Sending proper notification to the arbitrator.

2. Sending to the arbitrator the submission agreement (if the parties have agreed on the submission), and the pre-hearing briefs (if the parties have decided to use them).

3. Selecting suitable hearing rooms.

4. Arranging for enough copies of exhibits.

5. Considering use of reporter.

6. Setting the date for the hearing.

CHAPTER VII

PRE-HEARING MEETING

In some instances a pre-hearing meeting may have important results. If the parties believe that such a meeting could be useful in their particular case, they should arrange one. A pre-hearing meeting is an informal meeting prior to the arbitration hearing. Usually such a meeting includes the arbitrator and the representatives of the union and the employer. It does not include the witnesses. It may take place on the same day as the hearing but before it is officially opened; or it may take place on a day before the hearing.

During such meetings the parties may clarify the issue to be submitted to the arbitrator if this is a problem. And they could and should agree upon a written statement of the issue if they have not done so previously. The parties can discuss the facts involved in the dispute and stipulate to as many as possible, thus shortening the arbitration hearing. As for the use of witnesses, the parties could agree to limit their number; the parties could explore the possibilities of presenting the evidence in other forms, such as using depositions in place of witnesses; and also make certain that necessary arrangements have been made for the appearance of witnesses. Any other pertinent matters could be discussed and possibly settled at such a meeting.

In the case involving Mrs. Green and the Z Company, the parties have called a pre-hearing meeting with the arbitrator. The following report will demonstrate the use of such a meeting:

Clarifying the issue   ARBITRATOR: I have received the submission agreement from you gentlemen. Am I right in assuming that you are in agreement concerning the issues you want me to decide?

UNION: Yes, that's right. Counsel for the Employer

71

and I had a meeting in which we hammered that out. Do you think the statements are clear?

ARBITRATOR: If I understand them properly. Let's see, on this discharge-quit issue, you want me to decide first whether she quit or was discharged, and then if she was discharged, was the discharge in violation of the collective bargaining agreement.

EMPLOYER: Exactly.

ARBITRATOR: Is it correct that the employer is claiming that if Mrs. Green was discharged, it was for proper cause?

EMPLOYER: Yes, that's what we will prove.

Relief sought

ARBITRATOR: And the relief that the union seeks?

UNION: If you decide that Ann Green was discharged in violation of the terms of our agreement, then we ask that she be reinstated, with full rights as to her seniority and back pay.

ARBITRATOR: Can you stipulate to any facts on this issue?

UNION: No. Nothing. We don't agree on anything.

Stipulation on facts

ARBITRATOR: Are you sure? What about some of the dates involved? Don't you agree on the date of her employment by the company? The date on which the incident occurred? The date and time she reported back for work? The date of the visit of the detective agency shopper? And the dates of any meetings you might have had to discuss this dispute? Do you agree on where the incident took place and who was present at the time?

EMPLOYER: I think we could agree to those things.

ARBITRATOR: Well, why don't you get together and work out a stipulation on those facts, and any others you can agree on. If possible, file these with me in advance of the hearing. This will give me a chance to study them. Otherwise, file them at the hearing. We'll mark it as a joint exhibit. That will shorten the direct examination and will supply the record with basic facts. Otherwise, we'd have to take a lot of time getting these facts from witnesses.

> COMMENT: To stipulate to the facts means that the parties agree that they will both admit certain facts that are involved in the dispute. It is preferable that stipulations be worked out in advance of the hearing either at pre-hearing meetings with the arbitrator or at meetings between the parties and be submitted in writing to the arbitrator. But there are many occasions when stipulations will only be worked out at the hearing itself. In such instances they should, of course, be entered in the record if a verbatim record of the hearing is kept. (This is another reason why a reporter should be used at the hearing. If no reporter is used the parties should write the stipulations and submit the written statement as an exhibit.)

UNION: All right, we'll work out a stipulation on those facts.

ARBITRATOR: How about witnesses? How many do you intend using on this issue?

UNION: We're going to put Mrs. Green on the stand, of course.

EMPLOYER: We'll have Red Brown, the store manager. That's all I'm certain of at the moment. If we used more, it would only be one or two. There were no witnesses to the crucial conversation between Red and Ann Green, so we're going to have to rely pretty heavily on them for our evidence concerning this issue.

Effective date of ruling

ARBITRATOR: On this other issue, the one on sick leave, it's clear what you want me to decide in relation to Mrs. Green. Your second sentence in that issue says, "What shall be the application of Article 12 of the Agreement dated April 1, 1960, as this paragraph pertains to the three-day period?" What is to be the effective date of my award on this issue?

UNION: Well, we don't want to settle Mrs. Green's case and then have to fight each similar case separately that might come up in the future.

ARBITRATOR: Suppose I rule in favor of the union on this issue, would you come in with a lot of claims prior to Mrs. Green's and ask that they be settled the same way? In other words, are you going to try to apply this ruling retroactively?

EMPLOYER: We certainly don't want that. Offhand, I don't know of any identical cases prior to this one, but then we haven't reviewed the records with that question in mind. I don't want to run the risk that there might be some.

UNION: Don't get excited. We aren't asking that the ruling be given retroactive effect.

ABITRATOR: Then you'd better state what the effective date of the ruling on the interpretation will be. State that it will cover Mrs. Green's case and all cases subsequent to Mrs. Green's as long as the language of the provision remains the same, but will not be applied to any claims which arose prior to Mrs. Green's claim.

EMPLOYER: All right. I'll certainly see that we do that. I'm glad you raised the point.

COMMENT: Failure to agree upon the effective date of the interpretation of the agreement may lead to additional grievances that could have been avoided.

ARBITRATOR: What kind of evidence do you intend introducing on this sick leave issue?

UNION: The basic evidence is the collective bargaining agreement and you have that already.

EMPLOYER: We will want to establish the dates of absence and the reason for absence. I thought we'd use the personnel manager to testify to that. He has the records.

ARBITRATOR: Do you have any dispute on the dates she was absent?

EMPLOYER: I doubt it. We say they were May 1st (Friday), and May 4th (Monday).

UNION: We agree those were the days she was absent from work, but we say that she was out on the 1st because she was sick and was still sick on the 4th, so we would say she was sick from May 1st through May 4th, and was absent from work on her scheduled work day of this period, the 1st and 4th, because of being sick.

EMPLOYER: We're not arguing she wasn't sick on Saturday and Sunday. We just say Saturday and Sunday aren't included in the three days specified by Article 12 of the agreement.

Stipulation of facts

ARBITRATOR: It looks to me like you agree on the dates. Why not stipulate the facts as to dates and reason for absence and save us time at the hearing. And save money. After all, it costs something to bring in witnesses and my time isn't cheap, either.

EMPLOYER: That's all right with me.

UNION: All right. We'll make a written agreement right after the meeting today and send it to you right away.

ARBITRATOR: Will any other evidence be introduced on this issue?

EMPLOYER: I don't like to disclose my whole case but we do intend to bring in several witnesses who will testify as to past practice on this matter.

Witnesses: number to be used

ARBITRATOR: When you say several, how many does that mean?

EMPLOYER: There are at least 12 who could provide some information on it.

ARBITRATOR: Will they all testify to the same thing?

EMPLOYER: Just about.

Deposition or stipulation in lieu of witnesses

ARBITRATOR: Have you thought about using only one as a witness and getting depositions or stipulations from the rest which would indicate that they would testify to the same thing.

EMPLOYER: It did occur to me. But I think the union might object.

ARBITRATOR: The union would have notice that the deposition was to be taken and could be present to cross-examine or could submit written questions in advance. These persons will be under oath.

Depositions: their nature

COMMENT: A deposition is a written declaration under oath, made upon notice to the opposing party for the purpose of allowing him to attend and cross-examine the witness if he wishes to do so. The declaration is usually taken by an official person, such as a notary, or someone agreed to by both parties. The declaration may be in response to written or oral questions.

Depositions and affidavits contrasted

A deposition is similar to an affidavit which might also be used to introduce certain kinds of evidence in an arbitration hearing. The affidavit is also a written statement made under oath, but it differs from the deposition in that notice is not given to the opposing party as to the time and place for taking the affidavit as it is in the deposition.

Therefore, the other party has no opportunity to cross-examine. And this affidavit or other so-called signed statements should not be permitted to be placed in the record, except in extraordinary circumstances. This subject is discussed hereinafter.

UNION: We wouldn't object. But I don't see what you need to get depositions for anyway. We know what past practice has been. We aren't arguing about how it has been handled in the past. We're just pointing out what the agreement clearly means and how it should be applied.

ARBITRATOR: Well, now, wait a minute. You fellows have probably discussed this case quite a bit between yourselves before this meeting. Are there any facts in dispute that are relevant to the issue?

UNION: I can't think of any. I think we've agreed on the facts.

Presenting a case on written briefs

EMPLOYER: I'd go along with that. The thing we can't agree on is the interpretation of the agreement and its application to the facts.

ARBITRATOR: Maybe you should consider splitting this issue off from the quit-discharge issue and presenting the sick leave issue on written briefs. You would stipulate as to all relevant facts and then argue it on the written briefs.

UNION: That's possible. It would save a lot of time and money.

Why don't we get together and see if we can draft a stipulation of facts that would cover all the facts involved in the dispute, including past practice? If we find we really do agree on all the relevant facts, then maybe we could present the case on briefs.

COMMENT: Chapter IX deals with the presentation of an arbitration case on written briefs.

It can be seen from the above that the pre-hearing meeting may have several results. Lawyers will recognize the similarity to the pre-trial hearings. There is one connecting theme or purpose in all such results. The pre-hearing meeting is used to simplify, and to shorten, as much as possible, the arbitration hearing. It also helps to educate the arbitrator concerning the general nature of the case.

CHECKLIST: PRE-HEARING MEETING

To decide whether or not a pre-hearing meeting will be useful or to plan what to include in a pre-hearing meeting, all of the following questions should be considered:

1. Has the issue been agreed upon and clarified to the satis-

faction of both parties and the arbitrator? Have the parties stated all the issues they want settled?

2. Are there relevant facts to which the parties could stipulate?

3. Are there any arrangements to be made concerning witnesses?—as to their time or place of appearance?—as to limits on number of witnesses to be used?

4. Have the parties considered alternative methods of presenting testimony, such as depositions or stipulations?

5. Have the parties considered alternative methods of presenting the entire case—briefs or hearings?

Chapter VIII

PRESENTING THE CASE

The presentation of the case at the hearing is the climax of the arbitration proceeding. All the preparation which occurred at all stages of the dispute, the theories developed by the representatives, the investigations into the facts, were pointed toward their possible use at the arbitration hearing.

The hearing itself is conducted somewhat like an administrative hearing, with the arbitrator presiding. It has, however, more flexibility than a court trial, or administrative hearing, and can be more easily adapted to the type of a proceeding which the parties themselves desire or indicate. Thus, it can be legalistic or informal; strictly conducted or free-wheeling. But at all times it should be under control of the arbitrator. And he should conduct a hearing which is orderly, and designed to give both parties a full and fair opportunity to present their cases. With these principles in mind the hearing should be conducted with dispatch.

The following is the presentation by the union representative and employer representative of the case involving Mrs. Green. The parties have submitted one of the issues, the sick leave pay complaint, on written briefs. This presentation is concerned entirely with the other issue: Did Mrs. Green quit or was she discharged?

ARBITRATOR: This is an arbitration between Union and Z Company. This case involves Mrs. Ann Green. Are you ready to proceed, gentlemen?

UNION: We are ready.

EMPLOYER: We are ready.

ARBITRATOR: Do you have a submission agreement in this case, gentlemen?

UNION: Yes, we do.

Submission agreement and issue

ARBITRATOR: Oh, yes, I think this was the copy that you mailed me when I was appointed arbitrator. We will make the submission agreement Joint Exhibit No. 1.

I will read the issue for the record:

"Did Mrs. Green quit her employment with the Z Company or was she discharged in violation of the terms of the agreement?"

What about a copy of the agreement, gentlemen? You have sent me one of those, too, I believe.

All right. If there is no objection, we will mark this as Joint Exhibit No. 2.

EMPLOYER: No objection.

ARBITRATOR: All right. It has been marked. In this case the employer will present his case first.

Moving party and burden of proof

COMMENT: It will be noted that the arbitrator is asking the employer to open the case, or as it is usually called, to move first. The problem of which party first presents its case must always be distinguished from the problem involved in carrying the burden of proof. Ordinarily, when a complaint is filed, the party who files the complaint is referred to as "the moving party"

General rule

or the complainant. And in almost all cases it is the moving party or complainant who proceeds to present his case first to the arbitrator and has the burden of proof in establishing his claim. The other party or the respondent then presents his case, which is in the form of an answer or defense. And at that point the burden shifts to him to prove his answer or defense.

Special cases such as discharge

In certain types of cases, however, it becomes clear that the complainant or moving party should not present his case first. This is so in the instance of discharge cases. In a discharge situation, the employer has changed the status quo by terminating an employee's employment. Presumably he has done this for good cause, and the basis for such termination is within the purview of the employer. In an arbitration of a discharge case, therefore, the employer should move forward first because ordinarily the union is claiming that the reasons advanced for the discharge or the basis for the employer's action is unjust or improper or not in accord with the agreement. Since this is usually the claim of the union, it makes sense to have the employer move first and set forth on the record why he discharged the employee, i.e., the basis for the termination. Then the union assumes the burden to establish that the reasons or basis for the discharge were not proper or fair.

Unless this order is followed, it is quite likely that the union, if it moved first, may, when putting on its case, set forth what it believes or thinks were the reasons for the discharge. Then the employer would have to establish that the union's allegations were incorrect. The employer could only do this by actually setting forth why it discharged the employee in question. The result would be to complicate the record with two cases instead of one.

Therefore, in a discharge case, the employer should move first. Then he also assumes the burden of proof in his opening case to establish a proper basis, and the evidence supporting such a basis, for the discharge of the employee in question.

This burden then shifts to the party claiming that the discharge was unjust, to establish this claim on some relevant basis, i.e., that the facts relied upon by the employer were incorrect; that there was no violation of the agreement; that discharge was an unfair penalty, etc., etc.

In promotion cases

A similar situation could arise in a case where an employer has, under its agreement provisions, the right to select among contending candidates one of such candidates for a promotion and the union, under the agreement, has the right to challenge such a judgment. Again, in the interest of an orderly presentation, the employer should move first and assume the burden of proof to establish the proper basis for his selection. And of course the union, if it claims that the basis is improper, unfair or discriminatory, then has the burden of proving such a claim.

ARBITRATOR: (To employer representative): Do you want to make an opening statement?

Opening
statement

EMPLOYER: Yes, Mr. Arbitrator, I want to make an opening statement. I ask you to keep in mind the fact that there are two elements involved in this case: The discharge and the quit.

The agreement before you, which has been offered in evidence as Joint Exhibit No. 2, has within it this provision: Section 15 "The Employer shall have the right to discharge any employee for insubordination, improper conduct . . ."

There is also involved in this case a store rule, which we will bring forth as evidence. The store rule reads, "All sales people (and Mrs. Green was a checker-clerk in a grocery store) must ring up the full amount of each sale and hand to the customer the cash register receipt for such sale."

Bearing in mind the contract provision Section 15 of the agreement, which I have just read to you, and which I am sure you will review—and the store rules, which will come into evidence, the facts are simply these:

Mrs. Green was employed as a grocery clerk, working principally on the checking stand. The incident in this case involved the checking stand. During the morning of June 15, 1960, Mr. Brown, the store manager, told Mrs. Green to wash the windows in the front door. Mrs. Green, after a discussion at the check stand, rather reluctantly washed the windows, as I believe the evidence will show.

Thereafter, Mrs. Green came to Mr. Brown's office and engaged in a conversation with him in which Mrs. Green told Mr. Brown that she resented the manner in which he spoke to her in front of customers. Mrs. Green also questioned her obligation to wash windows under the terms of the contract, although she had washed the windows. This conversation, as is usual when the participants are a male and a female, deteriorated into an argument.

Mr. Brown, the store manager, said, "I also have complaints against you, Mrs. Green. You have not been ringing up sales properly, according to our store rule."

Mrs. Green got her back up on this. Her exact remarks will be brought out in the testimony, but in effect, she said to Mr. Brown, the store manager, "If you are charging me with being dishonest, I am leaving the store now." With that, Mrs. Green left the store.

She now claims she was discharged. Mr. Brown, the store manager, alleges that she quit. In substance, this is the issue. It is very clear; there is no question about it, and I am sure your decision will be in accordance with the facts.

UNION: Mr. Arbitrator, I trust that nothing the employer has said will be considered by you as testimony or evidence. It is so far from the facts——

Opening statement purpose

ARBITRATOR: I think we all understand that no opening statement is considered evidence or testimony. The opening statement is usually a presentation of counsel's most hopeful wishes that the case will go the particular way he describes it.

Does the union wish to make an opening statement?

UNION: Yes. In view of the way the employer has described this case, I think it is necessary at this time for me to make an opening statement. I will try to summarize the facts more accurately so that you will have a better idea of what will be brought out during the hearing.

This is a simple case of an employee with a fine record with her employer, the Z Company, with no adverse marks on her entire employment record. She was employed as a checker in a grocery store for three years.

The manager, Mr. Brown, has been constantly harassing her, attempting to get her to do menial duties, such as washing windows and that kind of thing, knowing all of the time that this employee, highly paid as a checker, should not be required to do that kind of work in the store.

Nevertheless, she has done the work and, as the employer pointed out, she did wash the windows on this particular day. Apparently, however, Mr. Brown was annoyed at the fact that she did not willingly submit to all of his directions which were made without regard to the terms of the agreement. Therefore, he started an argument with her after she had washed the windows.

In the course of this argument, Mr. Brown made further abusive remarks. Apparently it wasn't enough that he should abuse her, but finally he attempted to frighten her by saying, "And I have something else on you. I have a report that you have not been properly ringing up sales." This was said for the first time in this argument. She had no other notice of any dissatisfaction with her work.

This was the final blow, Mr. Arbitrator. As a result of this continuous harassment, this girl—and it is certainly understandable—broke down. She was beside herself, didn't know what to do, obviously couldn't carry on her work that day, so she simply said, "I have got to leave, I am sorry." And she left the store.

The next morning she came back to work at the regular time, and the manager said, "You quit, you don't have a job here any more. I have replaced you."

On the basis of those facts, it is clear that this was a discharge, a discharge without any basis under the terms of our agreement with the store.

Furthermore, we will show that the so-called store rules were never brought to the attention of this employee. She never saw the store rules. Nor was the union aware that there were such store rules, and certainly the rules had never been approved by the union.

Opening statements: desirability

COMMENT: Should opening statements be made? Generally it would seem to be a good idea to make an opening statement. It provides counsel an opportunity to outline his case, to state the facts as he sees them and to show how they fit into his theory of the case.

Ordinarily it is the first opportunity to acquaint the arbitrator with the dispute and the party's theory of it. It is obvious, therefore, that the opening statement should be carefully considered and stated.

ARBITRATOR: (To employer representative) : Will you proceed now?

Swearing of witnesses

EMPLOYER: A preliminary question, Mr. Arbitrator. In view of the union's opening statement, to which I listened with a great deal of interest and concern, I suggest that we swear all the witnesses today. We want to be certain that we are getting the truth.

UNION: I object to that, Mr. Arbitrator.

ARBITRATOR: There is nothing wrong with putting the witnesses under oath. Either side may ask that this be done, and in some states the arbitrator has the authority to administer the oath. The practice is that if the oath or affirmation is to be administered to the witnesses of one side, it will be administered to the witnesses called by the other side. We will put the witnesses under oath.

COMMENT: It has been suggested that requiring an oath lends more dignity to the proceeding and thus encourages the parties and their witnesses to conduct themselves in an appropriate manner.

EMPLOYER: Mr. Arbitrator, there are two elements in this case. We say that Mrs. Green quit and therefore was not discharged as the union claims.

Now, I know that if this were an admitted discharge the employer would have to "move first," that is, put on our witnesses and introduce our other evidence first.

ARBITRATOR: That's correct.

EMPLOYER: But this isn't an admitted discharge. We claim she quit. Who should go first in this case?

ARBITRATOR: The employer. The original complaint filed by the union claimed that Mrs. Green was discharged. Your contention that she quit is in the nature of a defense. We shall treat this as a discharge case. If you claim she was properly discharged, you must prove it; if you claim she quit, you must prove it as a defense to the complaint.

EMPLOYER: Who has the burden of proof?

ARBITRATOR: On the discharge issue, you have the burden of proof. And if you assert Mrs. Green quit, you have the burden of proof on that claim, too. The union must then try to show that you didn't prove your case. But if it advances any affirmative argument of its own it has the burden of proof as to such arguments.

COMMENT: The problem of who "moves" first was discussed in a previous note. The party who seeks to bring about a change (i.e., move away from the status quo) has the burden of proof to establish the validity of his action. Thus, in a discharge case, it must be viewed that the employer sought to bring about a change when he discharged an employee. And when he is challenged as to this action, the employer has the burden of proof to establish a valid cause for the discharge. This, in turn, is controlled by the terms of the agreement.

It will be noted that burden of proof includes the need to persuade the arbitrator that the action taken was valid and the requirement to produce evidence to support such attempted persuasion.

The union will seek to rebut the contention of the

employer. It does not, at this point, have any "burden of proof." It simply seeks to establish that the evidence offered by the employer in support of the discharge is not persuasive enough.

But if the union advances affirmative arguments against discharge such as claiming discrimination for union activity, or that others were not discharged in similar circumstances, then the union has the "burden of proof" to establish those contentions. Again it will be noted that since the union is affirmatively asserting a position it has the burden to persuade and offer evidence in support of such attempted persuasions. And the employer then may seek to rebut these contentions. In short, each party who advances affirmative propositions in support of its position has the "burden of proof" as to those propositions; the requirement to persuade that its position is correct and supported by adequate evidence.

In discharge cases the union often may admit the facts upon which the employer has acted. But the union then argues that discharge is too severe a disciplinary action for the alleged "crimes" committed. Stated in terms of a cliche: "The punishment should fit the crime"; or considering the crime, discharge which is "economic capital punishment" is too severe a punishment. The union, in effect, is suggesting that something less than discharge would be in order. Here again the union has the "burden of proof."

ARBITRATOR: All right. Proceed.

EMPLOYER: You already have in evidence the agreement, Mr. Arbitrator. I would like to call as my first witness the store manager, Mr. Brown.

ARBITRATOR: All right. The arbitrator has administered the oath. The reporter will note that for the record.

COMMENT: The purpose of direct examination is to place before the arbitrator by means of questions and answers the evidence which the party hopes will support his contentions.

The direct examination should be organized so as to develop support for the theory of the case upon which the examining party intends to rely. It should be literally "direct." The examiner should have gone over the testimony with the witness so that he will know what questions to ask and what answers to expect. He should not repeat questions after having obtained a direct answer to a question. There is no purpose served by repetition. If the party wishes to emphasize some fact brought out in the testimony, he should reserve that emphasis for his closing argument or summarization to the arbitrator.

The direct examination should be used to prove the examiner's own case. Opponent's arguments should not be anticipated by attempting to establish defenses before the arguments are made. There will be an opportunity to answer opponent's case after the opposing party has presented it.

EMPLOYER: Would you please give your full name, Mr. Brown?

BROWN: Red Brown.

EMPLOYER: And for whom do you work, Mr. Brown?

BROWN: I work for the Z Grocery Company.

EMPLOYER: Mr. Brown, this is an informal proceeding, do you mind if I call you Red?

BROWN: No. Everybody calls me Red.

EMPLOYER: All right. Tell us how long you have been working for the Z Company?

BROWN: Oh, let me see. I'd say maybe 15 or 16 years.

EMPLOYER: And what positions have you had in the company?

BROWN: I started first in the warehouse. Then I became a clerk and then I became manager of a store. That's what I do now.

EMPLOYER: At one time, were you a member of this union involved in this case?

BROWN: Yes.

EMPLOYER: And how long have you been a manager of this particular store involved in this incident?

BROWN: I've been there about four and a half years.

EMPLOYER: Now, do you recall the incident that occurred on June 15, 1960, involving Mrs. Green?

BROWN: I sure do.

EMPLOYER: Do you recall what time Mrs. Green came to work that day?

BROWN: Her shift started at 8:00 o'clock in the morning.

EMPLOYER: Did you see her come to work that day?

BROWN: Oh, yes. See, there's only a couple, two or three clerks, except on Saturdays when we have some extras. It's not a big store.

EMPLOYER: Do you recall the first contact you had with Mrs. Green that day?

BROWN: It was just the usual thing. You know, she came to work and she was working on the check stand, and we've got swinging doors in that store and it gets all dirtied up by the kids and I told her to go wash the windows.

EMPLOYER: Now, tell me, what did you say? Can you remember what you said to her? To the best of your recollection, use the words you used and the words she used.

BROWN: I told her to go wash the windows.

EMPLOYER: Just that?

BROWN: Yes. She knew what I meant. The only ones that ever get washed are those on the doors.

EMPLOYER: Did you say, "Go wash the windows" or did you say, "As soon as you finish your duties, Mrs. Green, I would like to have you wash the windows on your relief time"?

BROWN: There wasn't anything said about relief time. This wasn't during her relief time. This was during her regular time.

EMPLOYER: At the time you told Mrs. Green to wash the windows were there people waiting to have service from her at the check stand?

BROWN: No, no. It was a time when it was slow. Is that what you mean?

EMPLOYER: Yes.

BROWN: It was slow and we had another checker come on for the relief time. The relief hadn't started yet. So she and one of the other checkers were just standing around, so I said to Mrs. Green, "Go wash the windows."

EMPLOYER: What did Mrs. Green say to you?

BROWN: She said she didn't have to do it, she was getting tired of doing it. Because she had done it in the past. And she claimed that the union agreement didn't require her to do it.

EMPLOYER: What did you say to that?

BROWN: I told her it was none of her business what was in the union agreement. I told her she had to follow my orders and go wash the windows.

EMPLOYER: Did you say it in that tone of voice, in that manner?

BROWN: Oh, of course not.

EMPLOYER: Tell me what you said as well as you remember.

BROWN: I said to her very nicely—I said, "Now, look, it doesn't make any difference what's in the union agreement, you go ahead and wash those windows, they're dirty," and she says to me, "That's janitor's work." So, I said, "You wash those windows" and then I walked to the back of the store, because I had to get some cases. Part of my job is to fill the shelves and she came back and she told me——

EMPLOYER: Now, just a minute. Did you discuss at all her contention that she wasn't required to do that under the union agreement——

BROWN: I told her to go talk to the union about it.

EMPLOYER: Just a minute, let me finish my question. Did you explain to Mrs. Green in any way if she felt she didn't have to wash the windows she could ask the union to take the grievance up with the employer?

BROWN: I didn't tell her that. She's some kind of an officer in the union. She knows those things. Why do I have to worry about that? She was told to wash the windows and that's all there was to it.

EMPLOYER: Well, then, as I understand it, following that you went back to the back of the store?

BROWN: Yes. I went to get some cases and she comes tearing back there and——

EMPLOYER: Now, wait just a minute. Between the time you say she "tore" back there and the time you gave her the last instruction to wash the windows and you walked to the back of the store, were the windows washed?

BROWN: Yes, she washed the windows. She did do that. She went and washed them. Then when I was back there fooling with the cases, she came back and she was really riled up and still protesting.

EMPLOYER: And what was your disposition at that time?

BROWN: Oh, I was calm.

EMPLOYER: Well, now, who was the first to speak when she came to the back room?

BROWN: Well, she came charging back, like I told you. She tore back there and she says, "Look, I don't have to wash those windows. I'm not going to wash them any more. The agreement doesn't re-quire me to." And so I said, "Now, look, I'm not going to argue with you about what's in that union agreement. All I know is you have to wash those windows. And I want to tell you something else," I said, "We've had some complaints about you. The boss called me up this morning and told me that you haven't been putting those cash register tags in the packages at your check stand."

EMPLOYER: Now, let me stop you just a minute here. I want to get back to the conversation about the windows. Was that the sole conversation?

BROWN: Oh, that's all I can remember now. These are not exact words, you know. Time has passed, but that's my remembrance. Then I told her, because she was bothering me—the windows had been washed and I didn't want to argue with her any more—so I figured I might as well take the opportunity and tell her about this other thing.

EMPLOYER: And you told her then about not putting the cash register receipts into the packages?

BROWN: That's right.

EMPLOYER: And what did she say to that?

BROWN: Oh, she just got excited and she says, "You're making accusations. You're charging me"—— I said, "I'm not charging you with nothing. I'm just telling you what the boss told me." Then she got really excited and she got red in the face and she went and grabbed her coat and said, "I can't work here any more today," and out she went.

EMPLOYER: Now, let's stop there. Did she say, "I can't work here any more," or did she just say, "I'm leaving the store"?

BROWN: I can't remember the exact words, but I— I really don't remember the exact words but it was something like that. I know she was very excited. Maybe she did say—maybe she said, "I'm leaving," but all I know is she grabbed her coat and her purse and she just ran out of that place.

EMPLOYER: What were you doing at this time? Were you standing up or were you sitting down?

BROWN: I was standing there. And I didn't know what to do when I saw her do that. After all, you know, she's been there for a long time and we've always gotten along pretty well.

EMPLOYER: What were her final words to you then? I want you to give me those words again to your best recollection now.

BROWN: "I'm leaving the store."

EMPLOYER: All right. Was that the last thing she said to you?

BROWN: That's the last I've seen of her until today.

EMPLOYER: When she picked up her coat and walked out did you say anything to her?

BROWN: I didn't get a chance to. She just walked out.

EMPLOYER: Would it be fair for me to say you were just flabbergasted by her conduct?

UNION: I object to that question. He's putting words in the witness's mouth. Let the witness answer the questions.

EMPLOYER: Did you come to the conclusion, Red, that she had quit her employment?

BROWN: Well, I sure did.

UNION: I will object to that question, too! The arbitrator is the person who will have to decide whether she quit or not.

ARBITRATOR: I sustain the objection.

COMMENT: The making of objections is proper, provided the objections made are not frivolous and have some important point to them. For example, it is well to object if the questioning is "leading" the witness, that is, in effect, stating the answer to the question and simply asking the witness to agree to that answer. Or if the witness is asked for a "conclusion" or "opinion" on the very matter which the arbitrator has the duty to decide. Or if the witness is asked about something clearly irrelevant and immaterial.

EMPLOYER: What did you do after that? Did you replace Mrs. Green?

BROWN: Yes. I called up the personnel manager and I told him what happened and so he said, "Well, I'll get you somebody else," because I needed somebody right away, and he did.

EMPLOYER: How do you replace employees? Do you know where the employees come from?

BROWN: I don't know those things. I think they get them from the union. I don't know.

EMPLOYER: When the employee came in did you ask whether she was sent from the other store or the union?

BROWN: I really didn't, because—I mean, the personnel manager takes care of that for us in our chain.

EMPLOYER: Now, what was the next contact you had either with Mrs. Green or any union representative with respect to this incident?

BROWN: Well, the next morning, Mrs. Green came in and reported for work and I told her—"Well, I'm sorry, Mrs. Green, we have filled your position. You quit the job yesterday and I called up the boss and he sent somebody over here so I can't put you back on."

COMMENT: Note that just a few minutes before Red testified that he didn't see Ann Green again after she walked out of the store as a result of the argument on the 15th. Now he says he saw her the next morning. Counsel should catch such inconsistencies and resolve them or it may weaken the credibility of the witness.

EMPLOYER: What did Mrs. Green say, if anything?

BROWN: She said, "I did not quit." And I said, "As far as I'm concerned you did quit. But if you're going to raise an objection you might as well know you were going to be discharged anyway, and you are discharged because you haven't been following the rules of the store about putting register checks in the packages of groceries."

So I said, "It don't make any difference if you want to argue you didn't quit or were discharged, you're out either way."

EMPLOYER: And what happened next with respect to Mrs. Green?

BROWN: I don't know. I guess she went to the union. I guess that's why we're here.

EMPLOYER: Did you attend any of the grievance meetings on Mrs. Green's quit?

BROWN: No.

EMPLOYER: Do the cash registers used in your store issue a customer's receipt?

BROWN: Yes.

EMPLOYER: What happens to these receipts?

BROWN: The clerk is supposed to place them in the customer's bag.

EMPLOYER: Do the clerks do this?

BROWN: They are supposed to. It's a company rule.

EMPLOYER: Is this a sample of such a receipt?

BROWN: Yes.

EMPLOYER: I offer this sample in evidence as Company Exhibit No. 1.

ARBITRATOR: Any objection?

UNION: No objection.

ARBITRATOR: This sample receipt will be marked as Company Exhibit No. 1. Please give one of the copies to counsel and the reporter.

Exhibits

COMMENT: Note that this is a company exhibit. The former exhibits were joint exhibits, which means that they are presented jointly and are a part of the case of both parties. Exhibits that are admitted into the record are evidence. This means that the other side has a right to cross-examine with reference to the exhibits.

Exhibits may consist of original materials such as letters, or joint minutes of meetings. Or exhibits may consist of copies of documents, such as copies of agreements, copies of personnel records, copies of grievance reports.

Exhibits may consist of summaries, tables, or charts, computed, or compiled from other sources. The sources might be questionnaires, government documents and publications, or court decisions. In such instances the original sources should be noted and should be made available to the opponent to check the accuracy of the computation, summary, or compilation. It is not expected that there is any right to go behind the original sources. Such sources are usually accepted without question. Of course, even though the source is accepted, one may still attack the result. For example, a party may criticize the method employed in constructing the cost of living index or the whole concept of the index, but the particular index for a certain date is not questioned in terms of the accuracy of the computation by the Bureau of Labor Statistics in arriving at the final figure.

Before offering several exhibits, counsel should, of course, first consider all of the exhibits in relation to each other to be certain that they can not be used to contradict each other, in part or in whole. It is conceivable that each exhibit may support the parties case and yet be inconsistent with one another. This tends to destroy their persuasiveness.

EMPLOYER: I show you this document and ask you, is this a copy of the company rules?

BROWN: Yes.

EMPLOYER: I offer this in evidence.

UNION: Wait a minute! I haven't seen these rules. The union has never agreed to them. I don't even know if Mrs. Green has even seen them.

EMPLOYER: I'm sorry. I should have first shown you the document. Here it is.

COMMENT: Exhibits before being introduced should first be shown to the other party. It may be that the other party wants to raise an immediate objection to their introduction in evidence, and this opportunity should be accorded him.

EMPLOYER: I'm not claiming that the union agreed to these rules. They are company rules. Let me ask Mr. Brown a question. Were these rules posted in the store?

BROWN: Yes.

EMPLOYER: Do you know whether Mrs. Green saw these rules?

BROWN: I guess so.

UNION: Do you know? Not, do you guess so.

BROWN: I never saw her read them. But she has worked there a long time and she knows that it is a company rule to give the receipts.

EMPLOYER: I offer this in evidence as Company Exhibit No. 2.

UNION: I object. There was no showing that Mrs. Green read them.

ARBITRATOR: I will permit this to come in as Company Exhibit No. 2. The objection is overruled. The witness testified that these rules were posted in the store.

EMPLOYER: Now, Mr. Brown, have you seen this document before?

BROWN: Yes.

EMPLOYER: This is an exhibit of Mrs. Green's criminal record on moral turpitude. And I will ask Mr. Brown whether he had——

ARBITRATOR: Wait a minute. Are you offering this now?

EMPLOYER: Yes.

UNION: I will object to this, Mr. Arbitrator, as being irrelevant, incompetent and immaterial, on the traditional grounds.

Use of objections

COMMENT: The use of objections in an arbitration hearing does not have the same purpose as their use in a court of law. In a court, counsel uses objections on various grounds (and usually on the classic grounds of irrelevancy, immateriality, and incompetency) to get the judge to rule out offensive evidence on the theory that such excluded evidence will not be heard by the jury and thereby adversely prejudice the members of the jury. Often, of course, the jury will have already heard the ruled-out evidence, and it is quite possible that even though it is officially ruled out it will influence their decision in the case. The most important use of any objection in a court trial is to reserve the right to appeal if the ruling is adverse to the objecting party.

In arbitration hearings, there is no similar purpose for the making of objections. It has already been noted that the ordinary rules of evidence do not apply in an arbitration proceeding. And, ordinarily, there is no basis for appeal from an arbitration ruling to another level of arbitration or to a court on the ground that inadmissable evidence was permitted into the record. But objections wisely used do have a place in an arbitration proceeding. The most significant use is to test the question of relevancy if the objector believes the evidence or testimony offered is not relevant to the issue. Objections may also be used to keep the record from being "cluttered up." They may be used as a signal to the arbitrator, when he is studying the record, that in the opinion of the objecting party that particular evidence is either irrelevant entirely or entitled to very little weight.

However, often in arbitration hearings offered evidence is objected to on the ground that it is "irrelevant, incompetent, and immaterial." What is meant is this: Evidence is irrelevant if it does not relate to or bear on the points or facts in issue. It is incompetent if the evidence itself is of the type that is inadmissible, such as hearsay or opinion evidence. It is immaterial if, even relevant and competent, it is of such little significance or importance that it could not aid in resolving the issues.

UNION: There is no issue in this arbitration involving Mrs. Green's alleged moral turpitude, and I don't know how Mr. Brown knew about this anyway.

EMPLOYER: Mr. Arbitrator, I put this in because the evidence will show that Mr. Brown had this in mind when he discharged her.

UNION: Had what in mind?

EMPLOYER: This moral turpitude.

ARBITRATOR: Just a moment. You said that he had it in mind when "he discharged her."

EMPLOYER: If you would read that, you'd have it in mind, too.

ARBITRATOR: I don't intend to clutter up the record with this huge document unless this is admissible. When Mrs. Green was discharged, was she told that this was one of the bases for discharge? Are you making that claim?

EMPLOYER: No. But it was in Mr. Brown's mind.

ARBITRATOR: I would suggest you put it back in your file. It obviously has no place in this hearing. What was in Mr. Brown's mind when he discharged Mrs. Green is not relevant. After a discharge, it is not proper to go over the employee's record with a fine tooth comb and bring up something that the company knew about for a long time but did nothing about. There is no evidence that this record was one of the reasons for the present discharge. This does not constitute a warning which had been properly issued and would now be entitled to weight. It would be most unfair to permit the employer to drag an exhibit into the case raising a question of moral turpitude when it apparently never played a part in the discharge.

EMPLOYER: That's all on Mr. Brown, then.

COMMENT: As a general proposition, an employee who has been discharged is entitled to have his case heard on the specific facts used by his employer as the basis for the discharge. Put another way: Employer A decides to discharge X. He makes up his mind at the time he discharges the employee because of certain facts known or which had been made known to the employee. It is those facts which are placed on the table if the employee decided to appeal the discharge, and the case gets to arbitration. If arbitration results, the employer may not in fairness add at that time other facts or incidents which were not part of the actual basis upon which he formed his final decision to discharge the employee.

In fact, the best practice is to give to the employee (and in some cases the union) at the time of discharge a written statement of the reasons for the discharge. If the employer puts the basis for discharge in writing, it will give him a chance to evaluate the fairness of his action. Upon examination, he may find that the reasons do not justify the discharge. He is then in a position to reinstate the employee and avoid costly and unnecessary arbitration.

ARBITRATOR: Cross-examination?

UNION: Yes. I would like to ask Mr. Brown a few questions. Mr. Brown, would you state exactly the words used by Mrs. Green when she left the store after the incident on June 10th?

BROWN: She said, "I can't work here any more."

UNION: At another time in this hearing didn't you also testify that Mrs. Green simply said, "I'm leaving"?

BROWN: No. I didn't say that. She never said that.

UNION: Well, we will let the record speak for itself.

COMMENT: A verbatim record is extremely valuable in such instances. On this point, it will be remembered that Mr. Brown testified previously that Mrs. Green said, "I can't work here any more today," and then after further questions concerning the exact words he testified that she might have said, "I'm leaving."

UNION: No further questions, Mr. Arbitrator.

Cross examination

COMMENT: Cross-examination refers to the examination of a witness by the other party. Its purpose is to examine the witness upon the evidence given during the direct examination, to test the truth of that evidence, or to further develop it or clarify it.

Although the opportunity to cross-examine witnesses should always be provided, this does not mean that it is always advisable for the opposing party to cross-examine the witness. It has been asserted that the first rule of cross-examination is "Don't cross-examine unless you know the answers to the questions you intend to ask the witness." But there are times when cross-examination is useful. Maybe it appears that the witness is exaggerating or at least skirting around the basic fact, and this should be developed by a few concise questions. There is no doubt that the cross-examining party may materially weaken his case by overusing the tool of cross-examination. Some advocates have a notion that the way to cross-examine is to take the witness over the same ground covered in direct examination. When this is done, it gives the witness the opportunity to restate his case all over again, thus further fixing his direct testimony in the mind of the arbitrator. By this time the witness may have become more comfortable in his role as a witness. And in his more relaxed state may suddenly remember more details favorable to his side of the case. Or the cross-examination itself may serve to jar a witness's memory adverse to the case of the cross-examiner.

One further point on cross-examination: if the opposing party has any doubts about cross-examination, he should not cross-examine the witness. It is far better if he tries to win the case through his own evidence, and own witnesses, rather than through adverse witnesses. No one should go into an arbitration hearing depending solely upon the use of adverse witnesses to strengthen or win his case.

ARBITRATOR: (To employer representative) :   Proceed.

EMPLOYER: My next exhibit ties together the store rules and the cash register receipts that are in evidence with respect to Mrs. Green's violation of store rules. It is the report of the Detective Company. We ask that it be marked as the exhibit next in order.

UNION: I will object to that. There has been no proper foundation laid, no indication of where this report comes from, no opportunity to cross-examine the person who prepared the document. It is obviously not admissible.

COMMENT: This is an example of an exhibit for which the original source is the detective. The source must be produced for the opposing party.

EMPLOYER: Mr. Arbitrator, that report was discussed thoroughly in the grievance meetings. They all know about it.

UNION: Since you mention the grievance meetings, I would like to take this opportunity to offer the minutes of the grievance committee in evidence.

EMPLOYER: I object to the minutes. That is part of our attempt to settle the grievance through negotiation.

ARBITRATOR: Let's take these up one at a time. I need not remind you, gentlemen, that we are not in a legal proceeding and are therefore not bound by any of the ordinary so-called legal rules of evidence, even those dealing with the introduction of evidence. Nevertheless, we are bound by several important fundamental principles that apply in arbitration.

One is that evidence offered must have some relevancy to the issue. That is why I ruled out those so-called moral turpitude reports that the employer sought to introduce.

Now, I can see that the report of the Detective Company has relevancy to your claim that this lady violated the rules. But, the other party must also have the right and opportunity to cross-examine the evidence that comes in. Now, you can not cross-examine the document itself, but you can cross-examine the person or persons who drafted it.

Therefore, I would sustain the objection made by the union on this point. If you want to introduce the report, then you must produce its author. Then the union is in a position to cross-examine. Do you intend to bring in the witness from the Detective Company?

EMPLOYER: I anticipated I might have some trouble on this. My opponent is well known for making things difficult. He seems more interested in prolonging the hearing than in getting at the truth.

Stupid behavior

UNION: Wait a minute! Are you questioning my motives? I don't have to take that sort of thing. I could say a few things about you, for example——

ARBITRATOR: Now, gentlemen, let's remember that this hearing is concerned with issues that have nothing to do with any personal differences both of you may have—real or imagined. This hearing is going to be conducted in an orderly and dignified manner and will be confined to the issues before us.

COMMENT: This is a mild example of counsels nagging at each other. It should be avoided. Engaging in acrimonious behavior serves no purpose, except to clutter the record and try the patience of the arbitrator. Throughout the hearing the parties should attempt to develop the confidence of the arbitrator in their role as representatives. In part, this confidence results from his observation of the way the parties conduct themselves at the hearing. Any personal exchange between counsels will tend to destroy this confidence, and is, of course, irrelevant to any of the issues before the arbitrator. The attention of the arbitrator should always be kept on the case itself.

ARBITRATOR: Let's go back to this question of the Detective Company report. Do you intend putting the detective on the stand?

EMPLOYER: Well, I started to say that I had anticipated trouble in getting this report in, so I took an affidavit from the detective who prepared the report. The affidavit gives the information we need. I wish to offer the affidavit in evidence.

UNION: I object, Mr. Arbitrator. That is not the same thing as having the person here.

Affidavits as evidence

ARBITRATOR: I will sustain that objection. The trouble with letting affidavits and other signed statements into evidence is that it does not allow the opposing party an opportunity for cross-examination or a chance to properly rebut the testimony. I rarely permit such statements to be introduced, unless the opposing party agrees to let them come in. It's true that this is an informal hearing, but a line must be drawn somewhere. We can't make it so informal that the other party is denied the right to cross-examine or rebut the testimony. This could result in a failure of one of the parties obtaining a full and fair hearing.

And I should warn the employer representative that even if he persaudes me that there are extraordinary reasons for making an exception to the general rule and I allow this particular affidavit in evidence, I could not give it much weight. It is not subject to the same tests and scrutiny as other evidence.

Will you bring in the detective from the Detective Company?

EMPLOYER: I seem to have no alternative.

Grievance
procedure
minutes as
evidence

ARBITRATOR: We still have the question of whether the minutes of the grievance procedure meetings can come in as evidence.

As a general proposition, I will not permit the minutes of the grievance procedure to come in as evidence, because the minutes might contain compromise offers made by the parties in an effort to settle the matter. Compromise offers to settle the dispute should not come into the record. The parties might decide to settle the matter for many reasons other than on the merits of the case.

Compromise
offers as
evidence

Therefore, not knowing what is in these minutes, I would not permit them in. If the objectionable material is confined to certain sections, you may extract those sections and then show the minutes to the union, and then we will decide whether they should come in.

For the time being they cannot be accepted. If they are allowed in, they should ordinarily be used to refresh the memory of a witness or to impeach a witness. The minutes themselves are not proof of the facts but only evidence concerning what was said about them.

Shall we proceed?

EMPLOYER: Yes. I will call Mr. Jones from the Detective Company.

ARBITRATOR: He has been sworn.

EMPLOYER: Would you please state your full name?

JONES: Edward Jones.

EMPLOYER: Mr. Jones, is it correct that you work for the Detective Company?

JONES: Yes.

EMPLOYER: And what type of work does the company do and what is your job in the company?

JONES: It engages in several types of detective work. It has several stores as clients. My own work is connected with the stores. My job is to act as a shopper—to go into a store like any other shopper and to find out if the clerks are doing what they are supposed to be doing.

Sort of an outside check to see that clerks are ringing up the sales properly, not overcharging, giving receipts, and that sort of thing.

EMPLOYER: In the course of your work did you have occasion to make a check on the clerks at the Z Store?

JONES: I did.

EMPLOYER: In your most recent check at that store, what was the name of the clerk whom you observed?

JONES: Ann Green.

EMPLOYER: Would you please look at this report. Have you seen it before?

JONES: Yes. That is the report I prepared on the Z Store and specifically on my observation of Ann Green.

EMPLOYER: Mr. Arbitrator, I would now like to offer this report of the Detective Company in evidence.

ARBITRATOR: Does the union representative have any objections?

UNION: No objection.

ARBITRATOR: It will be marked employer exhibit next in order.

EMPLOYER: No further questions.

ARBITRATOR: (To union counsel): Cross-examination?

UNION: Thank you. Mr. Jones, at what time and on what date did you say that you were in the Z Store?

JONES: I didn't say. It's in the report. I was there about 10:00 o'clock a.m. on April 10.

UNION: How long were you there?

JONES: Oh, about 10 minutes, I guess.

UNION: Where were you during those 10 minutes?

JONES: Part of the time I was in the shelving section and part of the time at the checking stand.

UNION: How long were you at the check stand?

JONES: Long enough to have a bag of groceries rung up. A few minutes.

UNION: How did you know that the clerk observed was Mrs. Green?

JONES: They only have a couple of clerks there. I had their descriptions from the Personnel Department. It wasn't hard to tell.

UNION: How did you know that this clerk you observed, whoever it might have been, was not putting cash register tapes in the bags?

JONES: She didn't put one in my bag of groceries. You see, we pose as customers, get some groceries, then buy them like anybody else who is shopping, and observe closely to see that sales are rung up, prices are accurate, and receipts given.

UNION: Where were you standing when you were at the check stand?

JONES: Part of the time I was in line, but when the clerk was ringing up my purchases I was standing in front of her, so I could watch her and the cash register.

UNION: Did anyone else see this transaction?

JONES: Well, I don't think so. The store wasn't very busy. There were a few people in front of me, but none behind me.

UNION: As soon as you realized she had not put a receipt in, did you go directly to the store manager, so that he could check the package and verify that there was no receipt?

JONES: We don't do it that way.

UNION: How many other stores did you visit that day?

JONES: About eight.

UNION: Do you stop after each one and write your report on that store?

JONES: No, I usually do all my visits and then go back to the office and write my report from my notes.

UNION: Do you still have your original notes on the Z Store, Mr. Jones?

JONES: No.

UNION: How many stores did you visit after the Z Store, before writing your report?

JONES: I don't remember exactly. But from the time I was at the Z Store I would say about five others.

UNION: Isn't it a fact, Mr. Jones, that the companies expect you to file reports that show that your service is worthwhile, that you found something? Isn't it a fact that you are getting paid for being a stool pigeon?

EMPLOYER: Objection—I object.

UNION: I withdraw the question. No further questions.

EMPLOYER: Mr. Arbitrator, I offer now in evidence ten arbitration awards that I believe will be pertinent to your consideration of the legitimacy of the employer's position on this matter, and I will ask that they be marked as our next exhibit in order.

UNION: You are offering these in evidence?

EMPLOYER: I am offering these in evidence.

UNION: I will object to this. This is a matter of argument, Mr. Arbitrator, and counsel can put those in a brief if he wants to.

EMPLOYER: I am just trying to help you, Mr. Arbitrator.

ARBITRATOR: I appreciate the help you are trying to give. Are you suggesting that I am bound by those arbitration awards?

EMPLOYER: I will put them in evidence.

ARBITRATOR: I am asking you a question: Are you suggesting that I am bound by those arbitration awards?

EMPLOYER: Having gone over them very carefully, I will suggest that.

UNION: Naturally, he wouldn't pick out any other kind!

ARBITRATOR: That, under the agreement, I am bound by those awards?

EMPLOYER: No.

ARBITRATOR: You mean they are meant to be persuasive?

EMPLOYER: Very persuasive.

ARBITRATOR: Somewhere along the line you are going to argue this case and at that time you can refer to these arbitration awards. I can assure you I will read them all.

EMPLOYER: But we may reach the stage where we will submit the case without argument or briefs. What am I going to do then?

UNION: I would like to point out that I don't know under what circumstances these awards were made. I don't know the factual circumstances. Obviously they can't be controlling.

ARBITRATOR: They certainly can't be evidence. They are at best what in law practice would be called "points and authorities" in support of your position. They are not evidence.

And if you submit briefs instead of oral argument, you may refer to such awards.

COMMENT: Arbitrators should read awards referred to by counsel. Counsel should read the entire award before offering it. Too often only a part of the award is read which seems favorable to the case. But a complete reading may disclose material adverse to the case of the party offering the award.

EMPLOYER: All right. I will withdraw them. I believe that is all.

ARBITRATOR: You rest?

EMPLOYER: We rest.

ABITRATOR: Is the union prepared to go ahead?

UNION: Yes.

Before I call my principal witness, Mr. Arbitrator, just so you will understand what this so-called Detective Company report amounts to, I would like to introduce as an exhibit a newspaper clipping which I have here from a newspaper in another city of April 3, 1954, showing where this Detective Company——

EMPLOYER: Just a minute. Just a minute, Mr. Arbitrator.

UNION: I will offer it.

EMPLOYER: Before he characterizes it, I would like to see it. But first I would like to object to it.

ARBITRATOR: Look at it.

EMPLOYER: Even if I look at it I will still object to a newspaper clipping. It is hearsay. It is incompetent, irrelevant, and immaterial. Futhermore,——

ARBITRATOR: In the first place, the mere fact that it might be hearsay would not be enough to keep it out. It is clear that the union is seeking to attack the credibility of the Detective Company. For that purpose the evidence might be acceptable. But it relates to 1954; we have no way of knowing whether the branch in the other city is conducted differently than those in this city. We would have no access to any details of the 1954 case. Because of this the evidence is incompetent or even immaterial. That is, under the circumstances it is not significant enough to aid us in this arbitration.

Let's proceed, gentlemen.

UNION: As my first witness, I call Mrs. Ann Green.

ARBITRATOR: She has been sworn.

UNION: Would you please give your full name to the reporter, please?

GREEN: Mrs. Ann Green.

UNION: What is your occupation, Mrs. Green?

GREEN: I'm a grocery clerk.

UNION: How long have you been a grocery clerk?

GREEN: Oh, about ten years, I guess.

UNION: What was your last employment?

GREEN: I worked for the Z Grocery Store. I was a checker there.

UNION: For how long?

GREEN: I guess about four years.

UNION: Have you ever been discharged from any employment?

GREEN: You mean in the grocery business?

UNION: Yes.

GREEN: No.

UNION: Now, would you describe in your own words how you happened to leave your employment at the Z Grocery Store?

GREEN: Well, on this day—I've forgotten the date—I think it was referred to here already—I was doing my usual duties, and Red over there, the manager, came to me and he says, "Go wash those front windows." I had washed them before but every time I washed them I'd tell him I didn't think I should do it, that wasn't my work, that was the janitor's work. But he kept telling me I should wash them. I kept protesting. And then he just ordered me to do it and I told him then I didn't think I had to do it because the union agreement didn't say I had to do it and he told me—and he used pretty threatening language I thought, the way he said it—in effect, he said, "You better do it." So I washed the windows.

I guess I was pretty boiled up about it, so I figured if I washed the windows—I was going to tell him I wasn't going to——

EMPLOYER: Mr. Arbitrator, I object. If she wants to tell her story, I suggest she tell what was said at the time, not her impressions or ideas or how she felt.

ARBITRATOR: Mrs. Green, to the best of your ability, try to recall whenever you are talking about conversations the words that you used and the words that the other person used.

GREEN: All right. I'll try.

UNION: All right, proceed, Mrs. Green.

GREEN: Well, anyway, I was going back to tell Red, after I washed those windows, that I wasn't going to do it any more until the union told me I had to do it. He was in the back of the store getting some groceries to put on the shelves I guess, and I went back there and was very nice. By that time I was sort of cooled off. But right away he started giving me a bad time again.

UNION: What did he say?

GREEN: Well, this is what he said. He said, "I'm always having trouble with you about washing those windows and I'm getting sick and tired of it." Well, that got me excited again and I said, "Look, I washed the windows but I'm going to take it up with the union because I don't think I have to wash them." So he said to me, "Well, go take it up with the union." I was about to turn away to go back to the check stand when he says to me, "And there's one more thing," and I says, "What?" and he says, "I got a complaint from the boss today that you havn't been putting the register tapes in the bags of groceries." And I said, "Are you accusing me of being dishonest?" He said, "I'm just telling you what the boss said."

Well, after I had worked there so long, that just made me sore as the dickens and I just got excited and I said, "Well, I can't continue to work here today" and I grabbed my coat and ran out. I just got excited, that's all. You can imagine, working for somebody for so long and then having him saying that kind of thing about you.

UNION: Did you leave the store?

GREEN: Yes. I left the store.

UNION: And that, to the best of your recollection, covers the conversation and the incident that occurred between you and Mr. Brown?

GREEN: On that day, yes.

UNION: On that day. Now, at any time, Mrs. Green, did you say to the manager that you were quitting your employment?

GREEN: No. I wasn't quitting my employment. Why should I quit? I mean, I did my work. They never had any complaints about my work. I did get sore but you would, too, wouldn't you, if somebody made those charges against you? So, I just left, that's all, and the next day at my regular starting time I went back to work.

UNION: You reported to work the next day at your regular time?

GREEN: Yes.

UNION: What occurred that day?

GREEN: Well, Red was there and he said to me, "I can't put you to work" and I says, "Why not?" and he says to me, "Well, you quit," and I says, "I didn't quit," and he says to me, "Well, you certainly did." He said that, "You said yesterday when you left here, 'I can't work here, I'm leaving' or something like that." And I says, "Well, I never said I quit," and Red says, "Well, you better take it up with somebody else because I've got a replacement here already and I can't put you to work."

UNION: Did Red then tell you that you were discharged?

GREEN: He did not! He only repeated over and over again that I quit. Which I didn't.

UNION: Then did you leave?

GREEN: I had to leave. There was no point in standing around. I went to the union.

UNION: You took this up with the union?

GREEN: Yes. I told the union and they said they'd send the business agent to see Red.

UNION: Incidentally, Mrs. Green, have you worked since this incident?

GREEN: Well, it took me about two weeks to get a job but I've been working since.

UNION: You were out of work for about two weeks after the incident?

GREEN: That's right. And I couldn't afford it.

UNION: Now, as I understand it, when the manager told you about this, that he had this report that you weren't properly putting the cash register tapes into the bags, you became pretty upset. Did you?

GREEN: Well, sure.

UNION: Why were you upset?

GREEN: Because I always put them in there. I've been working for ten years as a grocery clerk and nobody ever had any complaints about me on that basis and nobody ever complained. Nobody told me I wasn't putting them in. That's like saying I'm cheating or something. That's why I got pretty upset. That's like calling you a thief. He didn't use that word, though.

UNION: But that was the impression you got? I mean, you felt that——

EMPLOYER: Objected to as calling for the opinion and conclusion of the witness. Her impressions make no part of this case.

UNION: I will withdraw the question.

Incidentally, Mrs. Green, do you know anything about any store rules in this store?

GREEN: Store rules?

UNION: Written store rules.

GREEN: What do you mean by store rules?

UNION: You remember the rules that Red identified earlier today as store rules?

GREEN: Oh, that. That's the first time I ever heard about store rules. I've never seen any around.

COMMENT: Arbitrators usually hold that the employer must give evidence that an employee is aware of any company rule upon which the dismissal is based. Some arbitrators have gone further than this and require evidence that the employee knows that a violation of a rule carries the penalty of discharge if discharge is in issue.

UNION: Were you ever warned prior to this incident about putting those tapes into the customers' bags?

GREEN: Well, I wasn't warned. I knew that you have to put them in. That's part of the duties of a clerk.

UNION: Were you ever told you were not doing this properly?

GREEN: No. Nobody ever complained because I always put them in. I know that's what you're supposed to do.

UNION: Had there been any other complaints about your work prior to this occasion except for this running argument that you apparently had with the manager about washing the windows?

GREEN: That's about the only thing I can think of. Otherwise, Red and I got along pretty well. He get's excited sometimes, but——

UNION: He gets excited?

GREEN: Yes. His hair isn't red for nothing.

UNION: All right. That's all.

ARBITRATOR: (To employer counsel): Cross-examination.

EMPLOYER: Mrs. Green, you testified that you always put the register tapes in the bags of groceries. Is that correct?

GREEN: Yes, that's right. I always put them in.

EMPLOYER: You can say then, without any doubt in your mind, that every time you made a sale you put the tape in the bag before giving the bag to the customer?

GREEN: Yes.

EMPLOYER: And in every case, you rang up each sale, put the money in the drawer, gave the receipt to the customer, before going on to the next sale?

GREEN: Yes, that's the way we do it.

EMPLOYER: Didn't it ever happen that somebody went by the sales desk with a candy bar or other small purchase and left the exact change for it by the cash register while you were ringing up another sale?

GREEN: The store doesn't like that to happen.

EMPLOYER: Well, has it ever happened to you?

GREEN: Not that I can remember.

EMPLOYER: Mrs. Green, if you always put the receipts in the bags, how does it happen that Mr. Jones of the Detective Agency did not get a receipt from you when he made his purchase?

GREEN: I don't understand that. He must be wrong.

EMPLOYER: No further questions.

UNION: I have a few more questions, Mr. Arbitrator.

Mrs. Green, you testified earlier that no one had spoken to you about violating any store rules prior to the discussion you had with Red Brown on the 15th of June. Is that correct?

GREEN: Yes, that's right. That's the first I ever heard any criticism concerning my work. Other than our window-washing disagreement.

UNION: In the four years that you have been at the store, you have never received any warnings about your work?

GREEN: That's right.

UNION: No further questions.

COMMENT: Arbitrators take the view that in certain types of cases an employee should be warned before he is discharged. These are instances in which the employee might be guilty of some omission, but the "crime" is not so serious as to warrant discharge. These warnings are intended to give an employee "another chance." When warnings are issued, they should always be in writing and, of course, given to the employee. If the warning is the last of several and if it is meant to be the "last chance," it should clearly state this fact.

There are cases, of course, where the cause of the discharge is so serious, that no previous warnings are required or are in order before resorting to discharge.

ARBITRATOR: Shall we proceed with the next witness?

UNION: I'd like to call the business agent of the union, Mr. Howard Smith.

ARBITRATOR: Mr. Smith has been sworn.

UNION: Would you please state your name and your position in the union?

SMITH: Howard Smith. I am the business agent for the union.

UNION: Is Mrs. Ann Green a member of your union?

SMITH: Yes.

UNION: Does your union have an agreement with the Z Company?

SMITH: Yes, we do.

UNION: How long have you had an agreement with it?

SMITH: For about five years.

UNION: Have you been business agent during this entire period?

SMITH: Yes, I have.

UNION: During that period did the Z Company ever discuss with you the so-called store rules which were presented as an exhibit in this case?

SMITH: No.

UNION: Mr. Smith, I want you to take a look at this exhibit, the so-called store rules. Please read it carefully. To your knowledge, has the Z Company ever discussed with the union these rules?

SMITH: No, there has been no discussion on these rules.

UNION: How many negotiations have you had with the Z Company?

SMITH: We've negotiated three agreements.

UNION: During any of these negotiations, were these store rules discussed?

SMITH: No, they were not.

UNION: No further questions.

ARBITRATOR: Cross-examination.

EMPLOYER: No questions.

COMMENT: The union is laying the groundwork to argue that the company rules are not binding because they were neither agreed to by the union or even discussed with the union. If the union should so argue, the company would probably reply that it has a right to establish company rules under the general authority of management to "run its business." And that such rules are binding, even if not agreed to by the union, so long as the rules do not violate the provisions of the agreement itself.

ARBITRATOR: Is the case now submitted, gentlemen?

EMPLOYER: Yes.

UNION: Yes, as to the testimony and exhibits.

ARBITRATOR: All right.

Now, gentlemen, what do you want to do? Do you want to make oral argument or do you want to file written briefs?

EMPLOYER: I am going to request briefs. I would want to analyze the transcript and submit briefs.

UNION: I would be prepared to argue this morning. I think it is clear. But since counsel has asked to file briefs, I will accede to that request.

ARBITRATOR: All right. If you had disagreed on that question I would have had to decide that point. And I would be inclined to grant the request for briefs, since one of the counsel desired to do so.

COMMENT: The parties are entitled to oral argument at the end of the submission of their evidence. If the parties prefer, they may waive their right to oral argument and submit at a later time their written briefs. Which procedure is advisable depends upon the nature of the case. If the case is complex and the record is long, some representatives prefer to have an opportunity to review the record before submitting their arguments. Or if the argument involves technical material, written briefs might be preferable to oral argument.

If the parties do decide they wish to present written briefs they should agree upon deadline dates for exchange of the briefs with each other and submission to the arbitrator. And they should agree upon time limits for rebuttal briefs, if any. If the parties desire the opportunity to examine the transcript, these dates are usually stated in terms of so many days after receipt of transcript.

Whether or not the parties argue the case orally or submit their closing arguments in writing, the arguments should have the same general content. It is in the arguments that the parties tie together the evidence submitted during the hearing in such a way as to support their respective positions. It is not simply a summarization of the case. It is a statement of the theory of the case supported by appropriate references to testimony and exhibits that give support and weight to the theory. This is the party's final opportunity to persuade the arbitrator that his view of the case is the correct view and his opponent's view is the incorrect view. It should be a carefully thought-out statement. No extraneous material should be included.

The argument should seek to give to the arbitrator such an analysis of the record that he could use it to write his opinion and decision if he is persuaded to adopt your view of the case.

Note: Additional references to closing briefs are made in Chapter IX—Presenting the Case on Written Briefs.

CHECKLIST: PRESENTING THE CASE

In presenting the case, the parties should keep in mind the following:

1. If a party wishes the arbitrator to put the witnesses under oath, he should request the arbitrator to do so at the beginning of the hearing.

2. If an opening statement is to be presented, it should be clear, concise, and well organized.

3. Exhibits should be presented during the course of the hearing. They should be shown to the other party first before seeking to introduce them.

4. If opposing counsel offers evidence that you believe should not be in the record, make a proper and timely objection.

5. The parties and counsel should avoid unnecessary friction between themselves at the hearing.

6. Direct examination should be to the point, complete but not repetitive.

7. Cross-examination should be used carefuly and only in situations where the advocate is almost certain that the testimony obtained through cross-examination will weaken the case of the opposing party.

8. Neither party should attempt to introduce irrelevant material into the record. It will not strengthen his case, and it may cloud the issue for the arbitrator. It also provides grounds for objection.

9. The closing argument should compellingly and persuasively present the party's theory of the case. It should be well-organized, and no longer than it absolutely needs to be.

Chapter IX

PRESENTING THE CASE ON WRITTEN BRIEFS

Presentation of an arbitration case through the use of written briefs should ordinarily be done only when the parties can stipulate as to all the facts with reference to the dispute. This means that the parties agree completely on exactly what happened; their dispute is limited to the application of the provisions of the agreement to the facts of the case.

If the parties can stipulate to all the facts, and do decide that they wish to present the case on briefs, they should:

1. Prepare a written stipulation of all facts to which the parties have agreed.

2. Agree upon and execute a submission agreement which includes a statement of the issues to be decided by the arbitrator.

3. Select and appoint an arbitrator for the dispute.

4. Agree between themselves as to the dates on which they will:

    a. exchange opening briefs.

    b. exchange rebuttal or closing briefs.

5. Decide whether or not there shall be a deadline date for the decision of the arbitrator. If there is to be a deadline date, the arbitrator should be notified of it at the time of submission of the issue to him and his assent obtained to such a condition.

6. Send to the arbitrator:

    a. copy of the submission agreement.

    b. jointly signed copy of the stipulated facts. If past practice is relevant to the case, it should be included in the stipulated facts. If there is no agreement on past practice, and it is a relevant fact for determining the submitted issue, then it is doubtful that the case is an appropriate one for submission on briefs. The statement of stipulated facts should include all facts necessary for decision of the issue.

c. copies of all agreed upon evidence such as the controlling collective bargaining agreement or agreements, reports on grievance committee proceedings, pertinent correspondence between the parties, and all other documentary evidence.

d. copies of the opening and closing briefs. These should be sent to the arbitrator simultaneously with their exchange between the parties.

In this method of arbitration the submission agreement becomes even more important than that in which the case is presented orally.

The submission agreement should include all of the following:

1. The agreement to arbitrate this issue.

2. A clear statement of the issue.

3. Appointment of the arbitrator.

4. Dates for exchange of all briefs.

5. Deadline date for arbitrator's award if the parties have decided that a deadline date is necessary.

6. A statement that if the arbitrator finds it necessary to obtain further information or to hear further argument after receiving all briefs he shall have the authority to call a hearing or to submit written questions to both parties.

Item 6 is essential in cases presented on written briefs. Often the parties believe that all facts necessary to the decision have been included in the stipulated statement of facts, but in reviewing the case for decision the arbitrator finds that something is missing. He must have the authority to obtain this additional information. His award must be based on a complete presentation of the case. Relevant information should not be excluded from his consideration simply because the parties failed to include it in their formal briefs.

A sample submission agreement for use in a case presented on written briefs is set forth in Appendix B.

It is difficult to make suggestions on the writing of briefs that will cover all types of cases. But some general statements concerning the organization of the brief and the material which should be included in it can be made. Opening briefs should include at least the following elements, and these elements should be stated in the order in which they are listed below:

1. A statement of the agreed upon issue.

2. A clear, concise statement of the position of the party.

3. The provisions of the agreement involved in the dispute, and analysis of those provisions in terms of the position of the party.

4. Application of the agreement provision to the agreed facts.

5. Argument based upon the party's analysis of the case. The argument should be directed in such a manner as to support the party's position as stated in 2 above. At this point the party should tie together the provisions of the agreement, the stipulated facts, his analysis, and show how all of them support his position.

The rebuttal or closing briefs should be concerned with replying to the other party's opening brief. It should not repeat what was included in the opening brief, nor should it introduce new evidence into the record. The reply should be an attempt to rebut the other party's analysis of the case and position. Specifically, in the rebuttal brief the party should attempt to refute the other party's application of the agreement to the stipulated facts or the emphasis which the opposing party put on certain of the stipulated facts. In other words, the rebuttal brief gives the replying party an opportunity to destroy or lessen the effectiveness of the opposing party's analysis and argument of the case. The rebuttal brief should be limited to that purpose and should not be used as an opportunity to reargue in an affirmative sense the replying party's own position.

Chapter X

ROLE OF THE ARBITRATOR

The arbitrator is the key person in the arbitration hearing. He conducts the hearing. He decides and rules on the admissibility of evidence. And he makes the final and binding award on the issues submitted to him. Clearly the advocates should constantly keep the arbitrator in mind during the preparation and presentation of the case. If the advocate wishes to win his case, it is the arbitrator he must persuade. His job of persuasion will be made easier if he understands the role of the arbitrator and has some insight into the way the arbitrator arrives at his decision.

Arbitrators will, of course, vary among themselves on the way they view their roles. Perhaps, however, some helpful information can be obtained by interviewing one arbitrator, recognizing that his answers will not necessarily apply to all arbitrators:

> INTERVIEWER: Well, Mr. Arbitrator, how will you decide the case of Mrs. Green? It's going to be pretty hard to try to satisfy both sides on this kind of case.
>
> ARBITRATOR: The function of the arbitrator is not to "satisfy" both sides. If the arbitrator conducts a full and fair hearing and makes a fair decision based on the record, that is all the parties have a right to expect of him. It may be that the arbitrator will be a "hero" to one side and a "bum" to the other side. But the party who may believe that the arbitrator did not do a good job need not select him again. That right is one of the important characteristics of the arbitration process.
>
> INTERVIEWER: Do you think in this case you could have avoided the necessity of making a decision by acting as mediator? Or do you think that an arbitrator shouldn't act as a mediator?

ARBITRATOR: I suppose if I had to say either yes or no to that question, I would have to say no. After all, the parties have asked for arbitration. If they had wanted mediation they could have asked for that. But sometimes, before the hearing is really under way, the arbitrator might realize that a certain suggestion from him might be agreed to by both parties. In cases like that, if the parties indicate that they are willing to hear the suggestion, the arbitrator could act as a mediator. It should be made clear in such instances that he is only offering a suggestion, and not indicating how he would decide the issue if the arbitration proceeds. But once the hearing starts in earnest he should not assume the role of mediator. In this case there was no indication that the parties wanted me to try to mediate the dispute involving Mrs. Green.

INTERVIEWER: That's right. It was clear that they wanted your decision. How do you intend to rule? Will Mrs. Green go back to work?

ARBITRATOR: I don't intend to write my decision during this interview. And certainly the parties have a right to see it before anyone else. After all, you sat in on all the proceedings. You should be in a good position to write the decision.

INTERVIEWER: It's true, I heard everything you did, but I've never been an arbitrator. Can you give me some idea of how you go about this business of deciding the case?

ARBITRATOR: Yes. First I will try to clearly understand the issue. In this case that's easy. Then I will study the agreement and the written briefs.

INTERVIEWER: What about the record in the case? (The "record" is used to mean the transcript, exhibits and written briefs.)

ARBITRATOR: That is the most important job. I will study it intensively. I go through the entire transcript, analyzing it carefully, making written notes on its contents.

INTERVIEWER: Exactly what do you do when you analyze it?

ARBITRATOR: Well, for example, the important witnesses in this case are, of course, Red and Mrs. Green. I will study their testimony to see where they agree and where they disagree. And where they disagree I have to "weigh" their testimony to see whose statements I believe. In this case the choice will be crucial.

INTERVIEWER: Yes.

ARBITRATOR: You will remember Red first testified that Mrs. Green said, "I can't work here any more." Then he wasn't too sure of that and testified that she might have said, "I'm leaving the store."

INTERVIEWER: That's not what Mrs. Green claimed she said.

ARBITRATOR: Yes. And Red said he later told her she was discharged. But Mrs. Green claims he didn't say this. This is contradictory testimony. I can't believe both of them. You can see that I will have to decide which one of them to believe.

INTERVIEWER: And from that you will decide whether she quit or was discharged?

ARBITRATOR: Yes. That's one of the first points I must decide. If she quit then the union's complaint that she was discharged was incorrect and that will end the case.

INTERVIEWER: Suppose you find that she was discharged?

ARBITRATOR: Then I will have to determine whether there was "just cause" for such action. What was the precise basis for the discharge? In this regard, I must decide whose evidence I will accept as to the posting of the house rules.

INTERVIEWER: Suppose you decide the rules were posted, or that in any case Mrs. Green knew as she admitted, that she is required to put the tapes in the package?

ARBITRATOR: Well, there is first a conflict in the evidence as to the tapes. The Detective Company said she did not put the tape in his package. Mrs. Green said she always put tapes in the packages. This evidence about the tapes must be considered carefully. Remember that the detective had no corroboration. He didn't immediately show the package to anybody else. It boils down to his word against hers. Of course, she might be expected to testify that she followed the rules. On the other hand, there is some suggestion in the record that because the detective was doing so many of these investigations and didn't write his reports until later, he could have been confused.

INTERVIEWER: Assume you believe the Detective Company's testimony, what then?

ARBITRATOR: At that point the evidence would add up as follows:

1. The Company rules were posted.

2. Mrs. Green saw the rules or knew about the tape rule.

3. She did not put the tape in the Detective Company's package.

That doesn't necessarily prove that she made a practice of not putting the tapes in the packages. The Detective Company's report relates to just one instance.

INTERVIEWER: What then?

ARBITRATOR: Then comes the tough problem. Does the evidence so viewed constitute "just cause" for a discharge? At this point the seriousness of the charges must be considered: the fact that no warnings as to the specific incident was given and the fact that no prior warnings were ever issued on this subject. After all, the punishment involved here is what we refer to in labor-management disputes as "economic capital punishment." Should this incident of breaking the rules justify "capital punishment"? The possibility that discharge for the cause stated was an "afterthought," that is, that Red was annoyed at Mrs. Green concerning the "window washing" episode and used the "tape" incident as an excuse to terminate her employment, must be considered.

INTERVIEWER: Couldn't the company argue that Mrs. Green was guilty of insubordination because she refused to follow orders and use that as a basis for discharge?

ARBITRATOR: Possibly. But it didn't. A review of the record will show that the company did not rely on that. If it had, the union might have argued that under the terms of the agreement Mrs. Green was not required to wash windows. A whole new question would have been opened and both parties would be expected to produce evidence on it. But this was not in issue. The company did not advance it as a basis for discharge and so I cannot consider it in my decision.

INTERVIEWER: Let's suppose that after reviewing the record you discovered that you need some additional information before you can decide. What do you do in a case like that?

Inadequate record

ARBITRATOR: There's only one thing that can be done. Get the missing information. This may mean calling the parties back for a further hearing, or if the information can be obtained in writing, I might direct written questions to both parties. But it is clear that the arbitrator has the responsibility to get the information needed for his decision.

INTERVIEWER: What if you realize during the hearing that the evidence is inadequate? Can you ask questions?

ARBITRATOR: I not only can, but I should ask questions if the needed information has not been supplied. If questions are asked, the arbitrator should limit his questions to both counsel and witnesses for the purpose of getting information. He should be very careful that he doesn't, by his questions or any other conduct, give one party or the other what may turn out to be false hopes as to the decision he finally makes. Both parties watch closely for any indications of the arbitrator's reaction to the case.

INTERVIEWER: When you write your decision do you put all of your analysis of the record into it?

ARBITRATOR: No, not as such. It certainly is necessary as to background. But there is no necessity to repeat the whole analysis. I try to write a reasonably concise opinion, setting forth the evidence which constitutes the basis for my decision.

INTERVIEWER: I have heard that arbitrators and even judges observe the principles of the "school of anticipatory jurisprudence." Can you explain that to me?

ARBITRATOR: Yes. That school proceeds on this theory: After a complete and thorough study of the record and issue, the arbitrator makes up his mind as to the conclusion he will reach on the issue. He then goes back over the record and drafts the opinion in accordance with his conclusion, drawing support for it from the record. Whether all arbitrators will admit this is the process followed is not in itself important. But the fact that this general mental process is used by many arbitrators either knowingly or unknowingly simply points up the tremendous importance of preparing each arbitration case adequately and completely. And in presenting the case the advocates should be certain that they have managed to get everything into the record that the arbitrator will need for his decision. After all, the arbitrator isn't playing a game of "eenie, meenie, minie, moe—," one for the union, one for the employer, etc. Nor is he seeking to compromise the issue. The arbitrator is deciding a case on the basis of the evidence and arguments introduced into the record by the advocates. It is up to the advocates to make that record complete—and to argue the case in such a way as to persuade the arbitrator that their theory of the case presented is the only sound theory, and should therefore be adopted in his decision.

INTERVIEWER: Does your opinion follow any set form?

ARBITRATOR: In a sense, there is a functional form that I usually follow. An outline of my decision with appropriate headings would ordinarily include the following:

The Issue

Position of the Parties

Events Leading to the Arbitration

Agreement Provisions

Discussion

Then, under "Discussion" in this case I would have a series of sub-headings such as these:

Did Mrs. Green Quit?

If I decide that she didn't, the next sub-heading could be:

What Was the Basis for the Discharge?

Company Rules

Did Mrs. Green Violate Company Rules?

Warnings

Summary

Under "Summary," I would set forth my final weighing (consideration) of the record and if I decide this is a discharge case then state whether under all the circumstances of the case there was "just cause" for the discharge. If I hold there was no just cause, then I will add a paragraph dealing with the terms of reinstatement and back pay.

INTERVIEWER: Does that end it?

ARBITRATOR: No, my decision or award is always stated in a separate paragraph or paragraphs labeled "Decision" or "Award."

The arrangement may differ from case to case, of course, but what I've just told you is generally the outline of an "Opinion and Award."

INTERVIEWER: I'm still curious. How are you going to decide this case?

ARBITRATOR: Well, as I said earlier, I believe strongly that the parties have the right to be the first to see my decision. I'll send you a copy after they have received theirs. But you don't need to wait for that. Now that you know the way an arbitrator approaches the problem, and you know as much about the case as I do, write your own "Opinion and Award."

APPENDIX A

THE ARBITRATION CLAUSE IN THE COLLECTIVE BARGAINING AGREEMENT

The parties to a collective bargaining agreement should give careful consideration to any arbitration clause that is included in the Agreement. It is always better for the parties to think through their own particular situation and custom-tailor a clause to that situation rather than just copy a clause from some other agreement.

The arbitration clause should include at least the following:

1. A statement that the parties agree to arbitrate certain types of disputes.

2. A statement that the arbitrator's award will be final and binding on the parties.

3. A statement that the parties agree to share the cost of arbitration in a certain specified way. The usual arrangement is that the parties share the arbitrator's fee equally. But the clause should be broad enough to cover other costs such as the cost of the reporter, if one is used, the rent for the meeting room, traveling expenses for the arbitrator, and other joint expenses which might result from presentation of the arbitration case. It is usually clear that each of the parties pays his own expense of counsel, travel for his witnesses, the cost of preparing exhibits, and the cost of his copy of the transcript.

Occasionally the agreement provides that the party who loses the case will be required to pay the entire cost of arbitration. Such a provision is based on the theory that this will prevent bringing frivolous cases or using arbitration as a means of harassing the other party. This type of abuse of the arbitration process is rare. And even if it were common, it is doubtful that this treatment of costs does much to deter abuse. This type of clause presents a further difficulty. In an arbitration case, it is sometimes impossible to say in precise terms who "won" the case. In any case, it should be remembered that the arbitration agreement is a mutual agreement and should receive support, including financial support, equally from both parties.

133

4. A description of the method by which the arbitrator is to be selected: The clause should also provide a method for selecting the arbitrator if the parties fail to agree upon a selection. Some agreements provide that if the parties do not agree, a named impartial agency (e.g., the American Arbitration Association or the Federal or State Mediation Service) should select the arbitrator.

It is in connection with this clause that the parties should carefully weigh the arguments pro and con about an arbitration board as opposed to an arbitration panel.

If the parties have agreed upon a permanent arbitrator or umpire, that person's name should be stated in the clause.

5. A clear listing of any procedural rules that the parties may wish to impose on the arbitration process; for example, this would be the appropriate place to set out time limits within which a request for arbitration must be brought, and within which the arbitrator should issue the award following the hearing.

The parties sometimes decide to be bound by procedural rules set out by associations such as the American Arbitration Association. If they wish to do this the procedural rules of that association may be included in the arbitration clause by reference to the rules and a statement that the parties intend to be bound by the rules of that association. If the parties do agree to this, it is important that they understand clearly and completely what is contained in the procedural rules to which they agreed. Occasionally a party agrees to be bound by the procedural rules of another organization or association without understanding the full impact of those rules.

6. A statement that the parties cannot move to the arbitration step of a grievance procedure unless they have first exhausted all of the other preceding steps. This is often implied by the language and structure of the grievance procedure. But a definite statement requiring the parties to first use the other steps takes care of any possible uncertainty on the subject. Of course, there are some cases in which the parties may wish to by-pass the earlier steps. To cover these situations the clause should provide that this requirement may be waived by mutual consent of the parties and that it can be waived by certain conduct of the party using this requirement as an objection to the arbitration.

7. An unequivocal statement that both the union and the employer may initiate the use of the grievance procedure including the arbitration step. Although this is generally understood without reference to the particular language of the agreement, there are some situations

in which strict interpretation of the agreement would deny the employer the right to initiate arbitration proceedings. This possibility can be easily avoided by including a positive statement granting the right to both employer and union.

8. In addition to the above minimum statements the parties should attempt to define as specifically as possible the type of dispute which will be subject to the arbitration clause. The parties may wish to strictly limit the types of dispute or matter which will be submitted to arbitration. Or it is possible that the parties wish to make the arbitration agreement as inclusive as it can be made. In either case it is clear that it is the language inserted in the agreement which will be the controlling language and will decide the issue—not the unstated intention of the parties. The following examples show how the scope of the arbitration clause may be broadened or narrowed in accordance with the wishes of the parties:

Assume an arbitration clause that reads: "It is hereby agreed that all matters relating to the interpretation and application of this agreement shall be submitted to arbitration." This narrow and restricted language grants to the arbitrator only the right to apply the agreement as written. If the parties wish to limit the arbitrator's powers to this extent, it is also advisable to add the following clause: "The arbitrator has no power to add to, detract from, or change in any way the provisions of this agreement." To be certain that a narrowly drafted arbitration clause will restrict the arbitrator to an interpretation and application of the collective bargaining agreement, as written, it may be necessary to incorporate in the agreement another clause which states, "This written agreement represents the entire agreement on all subject matters covered herein. Neither party has the right to request arbitration on any subject matter not specifically covered herein."

Assume an arbitration clause that reads: "It is hereby agreed that any questions or disputes arising during the term of this agreement, either out of the agreement or resulting from the relationship of the parties, shall be submitted to arbitration." Such language is a large grant of power to the arbitrator. Not only matters of interpretation and application of the agreement will be arbitrable but any type of dispute between the parties, whether covered in the agreement or not touched on at all in the agreement, will be submitted to the arbitrator as being within the scope of the arbitration clause. Under this type of arbitration clause it would be quite possible for the arbitrator to determine new terms of the agreement. For instance, if the agreement calls for a wage reopening clause and the parties cannot agree on the new wage rates, such a dispute would be submitted to arbitration as being within the scope of the language quoted above. And the arbitrator would have the authority to settle, and to make a part of the agreement, the new wage rates.

There is one further type of dispute which the parties should consider. Do they wish to include within the scope of the arbitration clause the question of whether or not a particular dispute is arbitrable under the terms of the arbitration clause? If the parties want the arbitrator to decide questions of arbitrability they should so state in the arbitration clause. The courts of most jurisdictions have ruled that, in the absence of an explicit grant of authority to the arbitrator, only the court has the power or jurisdiction to decide what is or is not arbitrable under a particular agreement. If a phrase granting that power to the arbitrator is included in the arbitration clause, then the courts are much less likely to attempt to take this authority on themselves. (For a discussion of the legal aspects of this question see Appendix C.) In view of the recent Supreme Court decisions, if the employer and union wish to restrict the type of questions which should be arbitrated they should be as specific as possible. An employer should not rely on a so-called management rights clause as a refuge against the possibility that arbitration will only be requested on matters specifically covered in the agreement. Although all questions which might be raised after the signing of an agreement cannot be foreseen, certain ones can be anticipated. For instance, if the parties do not want sub-contracting disputes submitted to an arbitrator, they should include an express prohibition to this effect.

It is difficult to overemphasize the importance of the language of the arbitration clause in the collective bargaining agreement or to overemphasize the danger of copying the language for this clause from any other agreement. The facts of each particular collective bargaining relationship are unique. An arbitration clause that may perfectly fit one factual situation could result in grave problems if used verbatim in another situation with different parties, a different industry, and different relationships.

Without the arbitratiton clause the arbitrator has no authority. All of his authority flows from that clause. The extent and nature of his authority is strictly limited by the specific language of that clause. Because of this, it is absolutely essential that the parties consciously determine exactly what kind of authority and how much authority they wish to grant to the arbitrator, and then carefully draft a clause which will carry out these purposes.

SUBMISSION WHEN CASE PRESENTED
BY WRITTEN BRIEFS

If the parties decide to present their case on written briefs, special care should be taken in drafting the submission agreement, or as it is sometimes called, the stipulation for arbitration.

As discussed in Chapter IX, the submission in a case presented on written briefs must include the agreed facts upon which the case will be decided, and must spell out in detail the procedure for exchange and submission of briefs to be followed by the parties.

The following is an example of a stipulation for an arbitration by written briefs:

THE PARTIES:

Employer:

Holbrook Co.
200 - 6th Street
Seattle, Washington

Union:

Novelty Workers Union, Local 820
900 - 10th Street
Seattle, Washington

IT IS HEREBY STIPULATED:

1. That Local 820 of the Novelty Workers Union has raised an issue involving the interpretation of the collective bargaining agreement between said Local and Holbrook's Seattle Plant;

2. That the question raised by the Union is whether or not the Company has failed to pay employees working a three shift operation the amount due under the contract;

3. That the Union contends that the Company is in violation of Section 25 and Section 12 (f) of the parties' contract;

4. That the Employer contends the employees are being paid according to the terms and provisions of said contract;

5. That both parties have agreed upon James Smith to act as arbitrator;

6. That the matter will be submitted to arbitrator James Smith through briefs as follows:

    (a) The Union being the moving party will submit its opening brief;

    (b) Within ten (10) days from receipt of the Union's opening brief the Employer will answer;

    (c) Within five (5) days from receipt of the Employer's answer the Union will file a rebuttal brief;

    (d) Within five (5) days from receipt of the Union's rebuttal, the Employer will file its answering rebuttal.

7. That each party will pay all costs of presenting its own case to said arbitrator;

8. That each party agrees to pay a sum equal to but not greater than one-half (½) of the fee and expenses of the arbitrator;

9. That the arbitrator shall confine his decision to the issues set forth herein and that his award shall be based upon the matters contained in the briefs submitted;

10. That the parties agree that the arbitrator's award shall be effective upon the date rendered;

11. That the parties agree to accept and be bound by the award of the arbitrator;

12. That the parties agree that the following shall be agreed upon facts:

    (a) That a third shift is in operation;

    (b) That certain machines are being operated on all three shifts;

    (c) That no employee works more than eight (8) hours in any one shift;

    (d) That certain employees work a continuous shift and eat their lunch at the machines while said machines are in operation;

13. That the above outline of facts are the facts upon which the complaint and the issue arose.

THE ABOVE STIPULATION EXECUTED THIS......................day of..., 1960.

                HOLBROOK CO.

                By ....

                NOVELTY WORKERS UNION, LOCAL 820

                By ....

Enclosure: Copy of Agreement in question.

Appendix C

SOME LEGAL ASPECTS OF ARBITRATION

Types of Law:

In the United States, there are two types of law:

1. *Written law (Statutory law):* The Constitution of the United States and the Constitutions of all the States form the fundamental law of this country. All other law must be within the general policies established by these constitutions.

Enactments, or laws, passed by Congress or the state legislatures are called statutes. Acts of cities are called ordinances.

All of these, the Constitutions, Federal and State statutes, and ordinances, comprise our written law.

2. *Unwritten law (Common law):* This is law developed by courts. When the courts have no written law on which to base its decision in a particular controversy, it decides the case on the basis of custom and general principles of right and wrong. These decisions create precedents or rules, which are applied to similar future controversies. The body of law created in this fashion is spoken of as the common law.

Much of the American common law was derived from precedents established by English courts before the Revolution. American courts have continued to modify the common law through their decisions.

On any specific subject both bodies of law, common law and statutory law, must be considered. If there is no written law on the subject, then common law, as applied by the courts of the jurisdiction, controls the situation.

If there is a statute on the subject, then the statute and its court interpretations control the situation to the extent the common law has been changed. However, the statute may not cover all aspects of the subject, or it may apply only in certain specified circumstances. Because of this, it is often necessary to consult both common and statutory law.

Law is a volatile field. The law on a subject may be changed by the act of a legislature or by a court decision. This is happening every minute. The law on a particular subject must be checked for the latest laws and decisions on that subject. The summary of legal aspects of arbitration set forth below is a general summary only and is not intended to be an exhaustive analysis of the law of arbitration in any jurisdiction. And even its general validity is limited to the law as it was at the end of 1959. But it is designed to give some indication of matters in this field covered by law.

I. ENFORCEABILITY OF AGREEMENTS TO ARBITRATE

A. Under Common Law (non-statutory)

Under common law, either party may refuse to abide by his agreement to arbitrate at any time before the rendition of the award.[1] Even after the hearing has taken place and all the evidence has been submitted to the arbitrator, a party may refuse to be bound by the award if he does so before the award is issued.

Nor will the courts, without legislation providing for it, allow a party to use legal action to force the other party to comply with the terms of an arbitration agreement. In other words, under common law it is not possible to obtain specific performance of agreements to submit disputes to arbitration.[2]

B. Under Federal Statutory Law

1. *United States Arbitration Act.*

The United States Arbitration Act was passed in 1925 and codified in 1947.[3] Under this act, agreements to arbitrate were specifically enforceable.[4] However, the United States Arbitration Act specifically excludes "contracts of employment." Federal courts have disagreed as to whether this exclusionary phrase should be interpreted to include labor-management agreements to arbitrate, thus excluding such agreements from the coverage of the Act.[5] This question has not been resolved by the Supreme Court of the United States, but with the interpretation of Section 301 of the Taft-Hartley Act [6] there is no longer any real need to determine whether the United States Arbitration Act covers labor-management agreements to arbitrate, unless that act is amended to provide such coverage.

2. *Section 301 of the Labor-Management Relations Act of 1947.*

Section 301 of the Labor-Management Relations Act gives Federal

---

[1] Bacon Abridgement, Arb. B., Comyns Dig., Arb. D., 5; *Vinyor's Case*, 8 Coke, 82.

[2] *Red Cross Line* v. *Atlantic Fruit Co.*, 264 U.S. 109 (1924) , 44 S. Ct. 274, 68 L. Ed. 582.

[3] 9 U.S.C. Sections 1-14.

[4] Id. Section 4.

[5] Held: collective bargaining agreements are within U.S. Arbitration Act, *Lewitts & Sons* v. *United Furniture Workers* (1951) , 95 F. Suppl. 851. Contra: *Int'l. etc. Furniture Workers* v. *Colonial Hardwood Flooring Co.* (1948) , 168 F. 2d, 876.

[6] 61 Stat. 156, 29 U.S.C. Sec. 185.

District Courts jurisdiction over suits for violation of collective bargaining agreements in industries affecting interstate commerce. In 1957, the Supreme Court, in the *Lincoln Mills* decision [7] ruled that this section gives the Federal courts power to order specific performance of employer-union agreements to arbitrate disputes. The Supreme Court in that decision declared: "It seems, therefore, clear to us that Congress adopted a policy which placed sanctions behind agreements to arbitrate grievance disputes, by implication rejecting the common-law rules, against enforcement of executory agreements to arbitrate."

In the Lincoln Mills decision, the Supreme Court directed the Federal courts to fashion a body of Federal substantive law to apply to these cases brought under Section 301 of the Act. In cases brought after the Lincoln Mills decision, the Federal courts have begun building this body of substantive law. Holdings have made it clear that the arbitration award as well as the agreement to arbitrate may be enforced under Section 301;[8] that the award may be returned to the arbitrator for completion if it lacks certain figures which make it impossible to enforce;[9] that the question of procedural arbitrability is a matter for the court to decide, unless the agreement specifically states otherwise.[10]

The Supreme Court of the United States has rendered three major decisions on certain aspects of arbitration law to be applied by the Federal Courts in Sec. 301 suits. These cases are important, not only for the points of law determined in them, but also for the Supreme Court's statements of general policy and attitude toward labor-management arbitration. Because of their importance to this field the cases are reproduced in Appendix D.

C. UNDER STATE STATUTORY LAW.

Some states have no arbitration statutes of any type. In these states the common law doctrine discussed above governs enforceability.

Five states have statutes which expressly exclude collective bargaining agreements from the coverage of the arbitration statute.[11] And seven states have statutes which expressly extend coverage to such agreements.[12]

Other states have general arbitration statutes which do not expressly cover labor-management agreements to arbitrate. In some of these states, including California, the courts have construed the general statute in

[7] *Textile Workers Union of America* v. *Lincoln Mills of Alabama* (1957) , 77 Sup. Ct. 912.

[8] *Textile Workers* v. *Cone Mills Corp.*, U.S. Ct. of Appeals, 4th Circuit (1959), 268 F. 2d 920.

[9] *Enterprise Wheel & Car Corp.* v. *Steelworkers*, U.S. Ct. of Appeals, 4th Circuit (1959) , 269 F. 2d 327.

[10] *Brass Workers Union* v. *American Brass Co.*, U.S. Dist. Ct. East Dist. Wis., 1959.

[11] Arizona, Michigan, New Hampshire, Oregon, Wisconsin.

[12] Maine, Minnesota, New York, New Jersey, Ohio, Rhode Island, and Wyoming.

such a way as to make it applicable to agreements by labor and management to arbitrate disputes.[13] Other states have not as yet applied their general statutes to labor-management agreements.[14]

II. JUDICIAL REVIEW OF ARBITRATION

Although arbitration tribunals are not a part of the judicial system, there are several ways in which the arbitration agreement, procedure, or award becomes subject to judicial review. This occurs whenever there is an appeal to the courts for some action in connection with the arbitration. This step to the courts may occur before the arbitration hearing or after the award has been rendered. It may take either of the following forms:

1. *a suit for specific performance of an agreement to arbitrate.* We have commented above on the common law and statutory rules on this type of suit. Legislation permits a party to an arbitration agreement to obtain specific performance. Before granting it, the court must determine whether, in fact, the parties agreed to arbitrate the dispute. This type of determination by the court has given rise to a question concerning whether the court or the arbitrator determines the issue of arbitrability when it is clear that an agreement to arbitrate exists but there is an issue as to whether or not a particular dispute is within the scope of that agreement. It is a difficult question because the issue itself may be easily confused with the merits of the case. Theoretically, it would seem logical to limit the court's determination of this issue to the existence of the agreement between the parties. If the merits of the case must be decided to determine whether the dispute is arbitrable under the agreement, or if the entire collective bargaining agreement must be interpreted and applied, these would seem to be the functions of the arbitrator. Regardless of the theory, the courts have not been uniform in their treatment of this question. If a question of this sort is raised, the parties must carefully research the law in their jurisdiction.[15]

---

[13] *Levy* v. *Superior Court,* 1940, 104 Pac. 2770, *Greyhound Corp.* v. *Motor Coach Employees,* Wash. Sup. Ct., 1954, 22 LA 55.

[14] e.g., Pennsylvania.

[15] For an excellent discussion of this problem, see Summers, "Judicial Review of Labor Arbitration," 2 *Buffalo Law Review* 1 (1952) ; also Plaut, "Arbitrability Under the Standard Labor Arbitration Clause" (1959), 14 *Arb. J.* 51. The following are examples of the court's treatment of this problem:

    Internat'l. Assoc. of Machinists v. *Cutler Hammer* (1947), Inc. 1297 N.Y. 519, 74 N.E. 2nd 464;

    U.A.W. v. *Benton Harbor Malleable Industries* (1957), 242 F. 2d 536;

    American Fed. of Grain Millers, etc., v. *Allied Mills* (1949), 196 Misc. 517, 91 NYS 2d 732;

    Monument Mills, Inc. v. *Textile Workers,* U.S. Dist. Ct. Mass. (1957), 152 Fed. Suppl. 429.

2. *a suit on the arbitration award.* This suit has one of the following purposes:

    a. to enforce the award

    b. to vacate the award

    c. to modify the award

Regardless of the particular reason for the suit on the award, the same general rules apply concerning the degree to which the court can review the arbitration case in order to determine the validity of the award.

(a) *Enforcing the award*

Although the agreement to arbitrate was not enforceable at common law, the arbitration award could be enforced.[16] After the award was issued the contract was considered an executed contract and the courts would treat the award as final and binding on the parties in accordance with their agreement to arbitrate the dispute.

Ordinarily, the courts will enforce the arbitration award even though the arbitrator has made a mistake as to law or fact. The arbitrator, as a general rule, is the final judge of both law and fact on the issues submitted to him. In a leading case on this point the court stated:

"The award of an arbitrator cannot be set aside for mere errors of judgment, either as to the law or as to the facts. If he keeps within his jurisdiction, and is not guilty of fraud, corruption, or other misconduct affecting his award, it is unassailable, operates as a final and conclusive judgment, and, however disappointing it may be, the parties must abide by it."[17]

It has also been held that an award will not be set aside

— on an alleged insufficiency of evidence because this matter is not reviewable by the court.[18]

— for failure of the arbitrator to follow the legal rules of evidence where the parties had not indicated that they intended to be bound by such rules.[19]

---

[16] For an early American case in which the nature of common law arbitration awards was discussed, see *Brazil* v. *Isham* (1854), 12 N.Y. 9.

[17] Where a claim in the Submission to Arbitration can only be applied from the facts alleged, the Arbitrator's failure to consider it is only an error of judgment established in the absence of fraud or gross misconduct and is not subject to judicial review. *Supp.* v. *Barenfeld* (1949), 34 C 2d 515, 212 P 2d 233.

[18] *Pacific Vegetable Oil Corp.* v. *C.S.T., Ltd.* (1946), 29 C 2d 228, 174 P 2d 441.

[19] *Griffith Co.* v. *San Diego County College for Women* (1955), 45 C 2d 501, 289 P 2d 476.

In many state jurisdictions, where the enforcement of the arbitration award is covered by an arbitration statute, the procedure for enforcement includes formal steps that must be taken and time limits within which these steps are to be taken in order to enforce the award. Therefore, even though an award is enforceable under both common and statutory law, it is essential to investigate the statutes concerning procedural matters relating to enforcement.

(b) *Grounds for vacating arbitration awards*

Both statute and case law agree that an award, otherwise binding, may be set aside where it can be shown that the arbitrators were guilty of misconduct, where material mistake appears on the face of the award, or where evidence of fraud is present.[20]

Misconduct of the arbitrator may be shown by proving that the arbitrator is interested in the outcome of the dispute,[21] evidence of partiality, such as visiting the home of one of the parties during the dispute,[22] ex parte consultations with one party to the proceedings,[23] or an unauthorized personal investigation by the arbitrator.[24]

(c) *Grounds for modifying or correcting award*

Many arbitration statutes give the court a right, upon certain grounds, to modify or correct the arbitration award and confirm it as corrected. Because these grounds vary from state to state, the law on this point of the particular state should be determined if the parties contemplate requesting such a modification of the award.

Typical grounds for this type of court action may be found in the proposed Uniform Arbitration Act which provides that the court may correct or modify if it finds any of the following:

1) an evident miscalculation of figures or an evident mistake in the description of any person, thing or property, referred to in the award;

2) that the arbitrators have awarded upon a matter not submitted to them, unless it is a matter not affecting the merits of the decision upon the matters submitted;

---

[20] "When May an Arbitrator's Award Be Vacated?," 7 *De Paul Law Review* 236 (1958).
[21] *In re Miller* (1940), 260 App. Div. 444, 23 N.Y.S. 2d 120;
  Schwartzman v. *London & Lancashire Fire Ins. Co.* (1927), 318 Mo. 1089, 2 S.W. 2d 593.
[22] *Robinson* v. *Shanks* (1889), 118 Ind. 125, 20 N.E. 713.
[23] *Spitzer Electric Co.* v. *Girardi Construction Corp.* (1955), 147 N.Y.S. 2d 40, 286 App. Div. 40. But, compare California holdings contrary to this: *Supp.* v. *Barenfeld* (1949), 34 Cal. 2d 515, 212 P 2d 233; *Griffith Co.* v. *San Diego County College for Women*, 45 C 2d 501, 289 P 2d 476.
[24] *Brotherton, Inc.* v. *Kraelshumer* (1951), 8 N.J. 66, 83 A. 2d 707.

3) that the award is imperfect in a matter of form not affecting the merits of the controversy.[25]

These are only a few of the legal aspects of arbitration. It cannot be overemphasized that any problem of arbitration law requires careful research concerning the law of the particular jurisdiction as it stands at the moment of the dispute. And the philosophy or history behind the particular legal doctrine should also be known. It is possible that a thorough understanding of that could lead to a persuasive argument to change existing arbitration law on a particular point.

---

[25] Proposed Uniform Arbitration Act, Section 13.

APPENDIX D

STEELWORKERS v. AMERICAN MFG. CO.
Supreme Court of the United States

UNITED STEELWORKERS OF AMERICA v. AMERICAN MANU-
FACTURING COMPANY, No. 360, June 20, 1960

Full Text of Opinion

Mr. Justice DOUGLAS delivered the opinion of the Court.

This suit was brought by petitioner union in the District Court to compel arbitration of a "grievance" that petitioner, acting for one Sparks, a union member, had filed with the respondent, Sparks' employer. The employer defended on the ground (1) that Sparks is estopped from making his claim because he had a few days previously settled a work-men's compensation claim against the company on the basis that he was permanently partially disabled, (2) that Sparks is not physically able to do the work, and (3) that this type of dispute is not arbitrable under the collective bargaining agreement in question.

[PROVISIONS OF CONTRACT]

The agreement provided that during its term there would be "no strike," unless the employer refused to abide by a decision of the arbitrator. The agreement sets out a detailed grievance procedure with a provision for arbitration (regarded as the standard form) of all disputes between the parties "as to the meaning, interpretation and application of the provisions of this agreement."[1]

The agreement also reserves to the management power to suspend or

---

[1] The relevant arbitration provisions read as follows:

"Any disputes, misunderstandings, differences or grievances arising between the parties as to the meaning, interpretation and application of the provisions of this agreement, which are not adjusted as herein provided, may be submitted to the Board of Arbitration for decision. * * *

"The arbitrator may interpret this agreement and apply it to the particular case under consideration but shall, however, have no authority to add to, subtract from, or modify the terms of the agreement. Disputes relating to discharges or such matters as might involve a loss of pay for employees may carry an award of back pay in whole or in part as may be determined by the Board of Arbitration.

"The decision of the Board of Arbitration shall be final and conclusively binding upon both parties, and the parties agree to observe and abide by same. * * *"

discharge any employee "for cause." [2] It also contains a provision that the employer will employ and promote employees on the principle of seniority "where ability and efficiency are equal." [3] Sparks left his work due to an injury and while off work brought an action for compensation benefits. The case was settled, Sparks' physician expressing the opinion that the injury had made him 25% permanently partially disabled. That was on September 9. Two weeks later the union filed a grievance which charged that Sparks was entitled to return to his job by virtue of the seniority provision of the collective bargaining agreement. Respondent refused to arbitrate and this action was brought. The District Court held that Sparks, having accepted the settlement on the basis of permanent partial disability was estopped to claim any seniority or employment rights and granted the motion for summary judgment. The Court of Appeals affirmed, 264 F. 2d 624, 43 LRRM 2757, for different reasons. After reviewing the evidence it held that the grievance is "a frivolous, patently baseless one, not subject to arbitration under the collective bargaining agreement." Id., at 628. The case is here on a writ of certiorari, 361 U.S. 881.

[POLICY OF LMRA]

Section 203 (d) of the Labor Management Relations Act, 1947, 61 Stat. 154, 29 U.S.C. § 173 (d) states, "Final adjustment by a method agreed upon by the parties is hereby declared to be the desirable method for settlement of grievance disputes arising over the application or interpretation of an existing collective-bargaining agreement. * * *" That policy can be effectuated only if the means chosen by the parties for settlement of their differences under a collective bargaining agreement is given full play.

A state decision that held to the contrary announced a principle that could only have a crippling effect on grievance arbitration. The case was International Assn. of Machinists v. Cutler-Hammer, Inc., 271 App. Div. 917, 19 LRRM 2232, aff'd 297 N.Y. 519, 20 LRRM 2445. It held that "If the meaning of the privision of the contract sought to be arbi-

---

[2] "The Management of the works, the direction of the working force, plant layout and routine of work, including the right to hire, suspend, transfer, discharge or otherwise discipline any employee for cause, such cause being: infraction of company rules, inefficiency, insubordination, contagious disease harmful to others, and any other ground or reason that would tend to reduce or impair the efficiency of plant operation; and to lay off employees because of lack of work, is reserved to the Company, provided it does not conflict with this agreement. * * *"

[3] This provision provides in relevant part:
"The Company and the Union fully recognize the principle of seniority as a factor in the selection of employees for promotion, transfer, lay-off, re-employment, and filling of vacancies, where ability and efficiency are equal. It is the policy of the Company to promote employees on that basis."

trated is beyond dispute, there cannot be anything to arbitrate and the contract cannot be said to provide for arbitration." 271 App. Div., at 918. The lower courts in the instant case had a like preoccupation with ordinary contract law. The collective agreement requires arbitration of claims that courts might be unwilling to entertain. Yet in the context of the plant or industry the grievance may assume proportions of which judges are ignorant. Moreover, the agreement is to submit all grievances to arbitration, not merely those that a court may deem to be meritorious. There is no exception in the "no strike" clause and none therefore should be read into the grievance clause, since one is the *quid pro quo* for the other.[4] The question is not whether in the mind of a court there is equity in the claim. Arbitration is a stabilizing influence only as it serves as a vehicle for handling every and all disputes that arise under the agreement.

[FUNCTION OF COURT]

The collective agreement calls for the submission of grievances in the categories which it describes irrespective of whether a court may deem them to be meritorious. In our role of developing a meaningful body of law to govern the interpretation and enforcement of collective bargaining agreements, we think special need should be given to the context in which collective bargaining agreements are negotiated and the purpose which they are intended to serve. See Lewis v. Benedict Coal Corp., 361 U.S. 459, 468, 45 LRRM 2719. The function of the court is very limited when the parties have agreed to submit all questions of contract interpretation to the arbitrator. It is then confined to ascertaining whether the party seeking arbitration is making a claim which on its face is governed by the contract. Whether the moving party is right or wrong is a question of contract interpretation for the arbitrator. In these circumstances the moving party should not be deprived of the arbitrator's judgment, when it was his judgment and all that it connotes that was bargained for.

The courts therefore have no business weighing the merits of the grievance,[5] considering whether there is equity in a particular claim, or determining whether there is particular language in the written instrument which will support the claim. The agreement is to submit all grievances to arbitration, not merely those the court will deem meritorious. The processing of even frivolous claims may have therapeutic

---

[4] Cf. Structural Steel & Ornament Assn. v. Shopmen's Local Union, 172 F. Supp. 354, where the company sued for breach of the "no strike" agreement.

[5] See New Bedford Defense Products Division v. Local No. 1113, 258 F. 2d 522 (C.A. 1st Cir.).

values which those who are not a part of the plant environment may be quite unaware.[6]

The union claimed in this case that the company had violated a specific provision of the contract. The company took the position that it had not violated that clause. There was, therefore, a dispute between the parties as to "the meaning, interpretation and application" of the collective bargaining agreement. Arbitration should have been ordered. When the judiciary undertakes to determine the merits of a grievance under the guise of interpreting the grievance procedure of collective bargaining agreements, it usurps a function which under that regime is entrusted to the arbitration tribunal.

Reversed.

Mr. Justice FRANKFURTER concurs in the result.

Mr. Justice WHITTAKER, believing that the District Court lacked jurisdiction to determine the merits of the claim which the parties had validly agreed to submit to the exclusive jurisdiction of a Board of Arbitrators (Textile Workers v. Lincoln Mills, 353 U.S. 448, 40 LRRM 2113, 2120), concurs in the result of this opinion.

Mr. Justice BLACK took no part in the consideration or decision of this case.

STEELWORKERS v. WARRIOR NAVIGATION CO.
Supreme Court of the United States

UNITED STEELWORKERS OF AMERICA v. WARRIOR AND GULF NAVIGATION COMPANY, No. 443, June 20, 1960

Full Text of Opinion

Mr. Justice DOUGLAS delivered the opinion of the Court.

Respondent transports steel and steel products by barge and maintains a terminal at Chicasaw, Alabama, where it performs maintenance and

---

[6] Cox, Current Problems in the Law of Grievance Arbitration, 30 Rocky Mt. L. Rev. 247, 261 (1958), writes:

"The typical arbitration clause is written in words which cover, without limitation, all disputes concerning the interpretation or application of a collective bargaining agreement. Its words do not restrict its scope to meritorious disputes or two-sided disputes, still less are they limited to disputes which a judge will consider two-sided. Frivolous cases are often taken, and are expected to be taken, to arbitration. What one man considers frivolous another may find meritorious, and it is common knowledge in industrial relations circles that grievance arbitration often serves as a safety valve for troublesome complaints. Under these circumstances it seems proper to read the typical arbitration clause as a promise to arbitrate every claim, meritorious or frivolous, which the complainant bases upon the contract. The objection that equity will not order a party to do a useless act is outweighed by the cathartic value of arbitrating even a frivolous grievance and by the dangers of excessive judicial intervention."

repair work on its barges. The employees at that terminal constitute a bargaining unit covered by a collective bargaining agreement negotiated by petitioner union. Respondent between 1956 and 1958 laid off some employees, reducing the bargaining unit from 42 to 23 men. This reduction was due in part to respondent contracting maintenance work, previously done by its employees, to other companies. The latter used respondent's supervisors to lay out the work and hired some of the laid-off employees of respondent (at reduced wages). Some were in fact assigned to work on respondent's barges. A number of employees signed a grievance which petitioner presented to respondent, the grievance reading:

"We are hereby protesting the Company's actions, of arbitrarily and unreasonably contracting out work to other concerns, that could and previously has been performed by Company employees.

"This practice becomes unreasonable, unjust and discriminatory in view of the fact that at present there are a number of employees that have been laid off for about 1 and 1/2 years or more for allegedly lack of work.

"Confronted with these facts we charge that the Company is in violation of the contract by inducing a partial lockout, of a number of the employees who would otherwise be working were it not for this unfair practice."

[GRIEVANCE PROCEDURE]

The collective agreement had both a "no strike" and a "no lockout" provision. It also had a grievance procedure which provided in relevant part as follows:

"Issues which conflict with any Federal statute in its application as established by Court procedure or matters which are strictly a function of management shall not be subject to arbitration under this section.

"Should differences arise between the Company and the Union or its members employed by the Company as to the meaning and application of the provisions of this Agreement, or should any local trouble of any kind arise, there shall be no suspension of work on account of such difrences but an earnest effort shall be made to settle such differences immediately in the following manner:

"A. For Maintenance Employees:

"First, between the aggrieved employees, and the Foreman involved; Second, between a member or members of the Grievance Committee designated by the Union, and the Foreman and Master Mechanics."

*   *   *   *   *

"Fifth, if agreement has not been reached the matter shall be referred to an impartial umpire for decision. The parties shall meet to decide on an umpire acceptable to both. If no agreement on selection of an umpire is reached the parties shall jointly petition the United States Conciliation Service for suggestion of a list of umpires from which selection will be made. The decision of the umpire shall be final."

Settlement of this grievance was not had and respondent refused arbitration. This suit was then commenced by the union to compel it.[1]

[THEORY OF COURTS BELOW]

The District Court granted respondent's motion to dismiss the complaint. 168 F. Supp. 702, 43 LRRM 2328. It held after hearing evidence, much of which went to the merits of the grievance, that the agreement did not "confide in an arbitrator the right to review the defendant's business judgment in contracting out work." Id. at 705. It further held that "the contracting out of repair and maintenance work, as well as construction work, is strictly a function of management not limited in any respect by the labor agreement involved here." Ibid. The Court of Appeals affirmed by a divided vote, 269 F. 2d 633, 44 LRRM 2567, the majority holding that the collective agreement had withdrawn from the grievance procedure "matters which are strictly a function of management" and that contracting-out fell in that exception. The case is here on a writ or certiorari, 361 U.S. 912.

We held in Textile Workers v. Lincoln Mills, 353 U.S. 448, 40 LRRM 2113, 2120, that a grievance arbitration provision in a collective agreement could be enforced by reason of § 301 (a) of the Labor Management Relations Act [2] and that the policy to be applied in enforcing this type of arbitration was that reflected in our national labor laws. Id., at 456-457. The present federal policy is to promote industrial stabilization through the collective bargaining agreement.[3] Id., at 453-454. A

---

[1] Section 301 (a) of the Labor Management Relations Act, 1947, 61 Stat. 156, 29 U.S.C. § 185 (a), provides:

"Suits for violation of contracts between an employer and a labor organization representing employees in an industry affecting commerce as defined in this Act, or between any such labor organizations, may be brought in any district court of the United States having jurisdiction of the parties, without respect to the amount in controversy or without regard to the citizenship of the parties." See Textile Workers v. Lincoln Mills, 353 U.S. 448.

[2] Note 1, supra.

[3] In § 8 (d) of the 1947 Act, 29 U.S.C. § 158 (d), Congress indeed provided that where there was a collective agreement for a fixed term the duty to bargain did not require either party "to discuss or agree to any modification of the terms and conditions contained in" the contract. And see Labor Board v. Sands Mfg. Co., 306 U.S. 332.

major factor in achieving industrial peace is the inclusion of a provision
for arbitration of grievances in the collective bargaining agreement.[4]

Thus the run of arbitration cases, illustrated by Wilko v. Swan, 346
U.S. 427, become irrelevant to our problem. There the choice is between
the adjudication of cases or controversies in courts with established procedures or even special statutory safeguards on the one hand and the
settlement of them in the more informal arbitration tribunal on the
other. In the commercial case, arbitration is the substitute for litigation.
Here arbitration is the substitute for industrial strife. Since arbitration
of labor disputes has quite different functions from arbitration under
an ordinary commercial agreement, the hostility evinced by courts toward
arbitration of commercial agreements has no place here. For arbitration
of labor disputes under collective bargaining agreements is part and
parcel of the collective bargaining process itself.

[COLLECTIVE AGREEMENT]

The collective bargaining agreement states the rights and duties of
the parties. It is more than a contract, it is a generalized code to govern
a myriad of cases which the draftsmen cannot wholly anticipate. See
Shulman, Reason, Contract, and Law in Labor Relations, 68 Harv.
L. Rev. 999, 1004-1005. The collective agreement covers the whole employment relationship.[5] It calls into being a new common law—the
common law of a particular industry or of a particular plant. As one
observer has put it: [6]

"* * * [I]t is not unqualifiedly true that a collective-bargaining
agreement is simply a document by which the union and employees have

---

[4] Complete effectuation of the federal policy is achieved when the agreement contains both an arbitration provision for all unresolved grievances and an absolute prohibition of strikes, the arbitration agreement being the *"quid pro quo"* for the agreement not to strike. Textile Workers v. Lincoln Mills, 353 U.S. 448, 455.

[5] "Contracts which ban strikes often provide for lifting the ban under certain conditions. Unconditional pledges against strikes are, however, somewhat more frequent
than conditional ones. Where conditions are attached to no-strike pledges, one or both
of two approaches may be used: certain *subjects* may be exempted from the scope of
the pledge, or the pledge may be lifted after certain *procedures* are followed by the
union. (Similar qualifications may be made in pledges against lockouts.)

"Most frequent conditions for lifting no-strike pledges are: (1) The occurrence of a
deadlock in wage reopening negotiations; and (2) violation of the contract, especially
non-compliance with the grievance procedure and failure to abide by an arbitration
award.

"No-strike pledges may also be lifted after compliance with specified procedures.
Some contracts permit the union to strike after the grievance procedure has been
exhausted without a settlement, and where arbitration is not prescribed as the final
recourse. Other contracts permit a strike if mediation efforts fail, or after a specified
cooling-off period." Collective Bargaining Negotiations and Contracts, Bureau of
National Affairs, Inc., 77:101.

[6] Cox, Reflections Upon Labor Arbitration. 72 Harv. L. Rev. 1482, 1498-1499 (1959).

imposed upon management limited, express restrictions of its otherwise absolute right to manage the enterprise, so that an employee's claim must fail unless he can point to a specific contract provision upon which the claim is founded.   There are too many people, too many problems, too many unforeseeable contingencies to make the words of the contract the exclusive source of rights and duties.   One cannot reduce all the rules governing community like an industrial plant to fifteen or even fifty pages.   Within the sphere of collective bargaining, the institutional characteristics and the governmental nature of the collective-bargaining process demand a common law of the shop which implements and furnishes the context of the agreement.   We must assume that intelligent negotiators acknowledged so plain a need unless they stated a contrary rule in plan words."

A collective bargaining agreement is an effort to erect a system of industrial self-government.   When most parties enter into contractual relationship they do so voluntarily, in the sense that there is no real compulsion to deal with one another, as opposed to dealing with other parties.   This is not true of the labor agreement.   The choice is generally not between entering or refusing to enter into a relationship, for that in all probability pre-exists the negotiations.   Rather it is between having that relationship governed by an agreed upon rule of law or leaving each and every matter subject to a temporary resolution dependent solely upon the relative strength, at any given moment, of the contending forces. The mature labor agreement may attempt to regulate all aspects of the complicated relationship, from the most crucial to the most minute over an extended period of time.   Because of the compulsion to reach agreement and the breadth of the matters covered, as well as the need for a fairly concise and readable instrument, the product of negotiations (the written document) is, in the words of the late Dean Shulman, "a compilation of diverse provisions; some provide objective criteria almost automatically applicable; some provide more or less specific standards which require reason and judgment in their application; and some do little more than leave problems to future consideration with an expression of hope and good faith."   Shulman, supra, at 1005.   Gaps may be left to be filled in by reference to the practices of the particular industry and of the various shops covered by the agreement.   Many of the specific practices which underlie the agreement may be unknown, except in hazy form, even to the negotiators.   Courts and arbitration in the context of most commercial contracts are resorted to because there has been a breakdown in the working relationship of the parties; such resort is the unwanted exception.   But the grievance machinery under a collective bargaining agreement is at the very heart of the system of industrial self-government. Arbitration is the means of solving the un-foreseeable by molding a system of private law for all the problems which may arise and to provide for their solution in a way which will generally accord with the variant needs and desires of the parties. The processing of disputes through the grievance machinery is actually a vehicle by which meaning and content is given to the collective bargaining agreement.

[SCOPE OF ARBITRATION CLAUSE]

Apart from matters that the parties specifically exclude, all of the questions on which the parties disagree must therefore come within the scope of the grievance and arbitration provisions of the collective agreement. The grievance procedure is, in other words, a part of the continuous collective bargaining process. It, rather than a strike, is the terminal point of a disagreement.

"A proper conception of the arbitrator's function is basic. He is not a public tribunal imposed upon the parties by superior authority which the parties are obliged to accept. He has no general charter to administer justice for a community which transcends the parties. He is rather part of a system of self-government created by and confined to the parties * * *" Shulman, supra, at 1016.

The labor arbitrator performs functions which are not normal to the courts; the considerations which help him fashion judgments may indeed be foreign to the competence of courts. The labor arbitrator's source of law is not confined to the express provisions of the contract, as the industrial common law—the practices of the industry and the shop—is equally a part of the collective bargaining agreement although not expressed in it. The labor arbitrator is usually chosen because of the parties' confidence in his knowledge of the common law of the shop and their trust in his personal judgment to bring to bear considerations which are not expressed in the contract as criteria for judgment. The parties expect that his judgment of a particular grievance will reflect not only what the contract says but, insofar as the collective bargaining agreement permits, such factors as the effect upon productivity of a particular result, its consequence to the morale of the shop, his judgment whether tensions will be heightened or diminished. For the parties' objective in using the arbitration process is primarily to further their common goal of uninterrupted production under the agreement to make the agreement serve their specialized needs. The ablest judge cannot be expected to bring the same experience and competence to bear upon the determination of a grievance, because he cannot be similarly informed.

[JUDICIAL INQUIRY]

The Congress, however, has by § 301 of the Labor Management Relations Act, assigned the courts the duty of determining whether the reluctant party has breached his promise to arbitrate. For arbitration is a matter of contract and a party cannot be required to submit to arbitration any dispute which he has not agreed so to submit. Yet, to be consistent with congressional policy in favor of settlement of disputes by the parties through the machinery of arbitration, the judicial inquiry under § 301 must be strictly confined to question whether the reluctant party did agree to arbitrate the grievance or agreed to give the arbitrator power to make the award he made. An order to arbitrate the particular grievance should not be denied unless it may be said with positive assurance that arbitration clause is not susceptible to an interpretation that covers the asserted dispute. Doubts should be resolved in favor of coverage.[7]

We do not agree with the lower courts that contracting-out grievances were necessarily excepted from the grievance procedure of this agreement. To be sure the agreement provides that "matters which are strictly a function of management shall not be subject to arbitration." But it goes on to say that if "differences" arise or if "any local trouble of any kind" arises, the grievance procedure shall be applicable.

Collective bargaining agreements regulate or restrict the exercise of management functions; they do not oust management from the performance of them. Management hires and fires, pays and promotes, supervises and plans. All these are part of its function, and absent a collective bargaining agreement, it may be exercised freely except as limited by public law and by the willingness of employees to work under the particular, unilaterally imposed conditions. A collective bargaining agreement may treat only with certain specific practices, leaving the rest to management but subject to the possibility of work stoppages. When, however, an absolute no-strike clause is included in the agreement, then in a very real sense everything that management does is subject to the agreement, for either management is prohibited or limited in the action it takes, or if not, it is protected from interference by strikes. This comprehensive reach of the collective bargaining agreement does not mean,

---

[7] It is clear that under both the agreement in this case and that involved in American Manufacturing Co., ante. p.—, 48 LRRM 2414, the question of arbitrability is for the courts to decide. Cf. Cox, Reflections Upon Labor Arbitration, 72 Harv. L. Rev. 1482, 1508-1509. Where the assertion by the claimant is that the parties excluded from court determination not merely the decision of the merits of the grievance but also the question of its arbitrability, vesting power to make both decisions in the arbitrator, the claimant must bear the burden of a clear demonstration of that purpose.

however, that the language, "strictly a function of management" has no meaning.

"Strictly a function of management" might be thought to refer to any practice of management in which, under particular circumstances prescribed by the agreement, it is permitted to indulge. But if courts, in order to determine arbitrability, were allowed to determine what is permitted and what is not, the arbitration clause would be swallowed up by the exception. Every grievance in a sense involves a claim that management has violated some provision of the agreement.

[FUNCTION OF MANAGEMENT]

Accordingly, "strictly a function of management" must be interpreted as referring only to that over which the contract gives management complete control and unfettered discretion. Respondent claims that the contracting-out of work falls within this category. Contracting-out work is the basis of many grievances: and that type of claim is grist in the mills of the arbitrators.[8] A specific collective bargaining agreement may exclude contracting-out from the grievance procedure. Or a written collateral agreement may make clear that contracting-out was not a matter for arbitration. In such a case a grievance based solely on contracting-out would not be arbitrable. Here, however, there is no such provision. Nor is there any showing that the parties designed the phrase "strictly a function of management" to encompass any and all forms of contracting-out. In the absence of any express provision excluding a particular grievance from arbitration, we think only the most forceful evidence of a purpose to exclude the claim from arbitration can prevail, particularly where, as here, the exclusion clause is vague and the arbitration clause quite broad. Since any attempt by a court to infer such a purpose necessarily comprehends the merits, the court should view with suspicion an attempt to persuade it to become entangled in the construction of the substantive provisions of a labor agreement, even through the back door of interpreting the arbitration clause, when the alternative is to utilize the services of an arbitrator.

The grievance alleged that the contracting-out was a violation of the collective bargaining agreement. There was, therefore, a dispute "as to

---

[8] See Celanese Corp. of America, 33 LA 925, 941 (1959), where the arbiter in a grievance growing out of contracting-out work said:

"In my research I have located 64 published decisions which have been concerned with this issue covering a wide range of factual situations but all of them with the common characteristics—i.e., the contracting-out of work involved occurred under an Agreement that contained no provision that specifically mentioned contracting-out of work."

the meaning and application of the provisions of this Agreement" which the parties had agreed would be determined by arbitration.

The judiciary sits in these cases to bring into operation an arbitral process which substitutes a regime of peaceful settlement for the older regime of industrial conflict. Whether contracting-out in the present case violated the agreement is the question. It is a question for the arbiter, not for the courts.

Reversed.

Mr. Justice FRANKFURTER concurs in the result.

Mr. Justice BLACK took no part in the consideration or decision of this case.

———

Dissenting Opinion

Mr. Justice WHITTAKER, dissenting.

Until today, I have understood it to be the unquestioned law, as this Court has consistently held, that arbitrators are private judges chosen by the parties to decide particular matters specifically submitted; [1] that the contract under which matters are submitted to arbitrators is at once the source and limit of their authority and power; [2] and that their power to decide issues with finality, thus ousting the normal functions of the courts, must rest upon a clear, definitive agreement of the parties, as such powers can never be implied, United States v. Moorman, 338 U.S. 457, 462; [3] Mercantile Trust Co. v. Hensey, 205 U.S. 298, 309.[4] See also Fernandez & Hnos v. Rickert Mills, 119 F. 2d 809, 815 (C.A. 1st Cir.); [5] Marchant v. Mead-Morrison Mfg. Co., 252 N.Y. 284, 299, 169 N.E. 386,

———

[1] "Arbitrators are judges chosen by the parties to decide the matter submitted to them." Burchell v. Marsh, 17 How. 334, 349.

[2] "The agreement under which [the arbitrators] were selected *was at once the source and limit of their authority,* and the award, to be binding, must in substance and form conform to the submission." Continental Ins. Co. v. Garrett, 125 F. 589, 590 (C.A. 6th Cir.) —Opinion by Judge, labor Mr. Justice, Lurton. (Emphasis added.)

[3] "It is true that *the intention of the parties to submit their contractual disputes to final determination outside the courts should be made manifest by plain language.*" United States v. Moorman, 338 U.S. 457, 462. (Emphasis added.)

[4] "To make such [an arbitrator's] certificate conclusive *requires plain language in the contract.* It is not to be implied." Mercantile Trust Co. v. Hensey, 205 U.S. 298, 309. (Emphasis added.)

[5] "A party is never required to submit to arbitration any question which he has not agreed so to submit, and contracts providing for arbitration *will be carefully construed in order not to force a party to submit to arbitration a question which he did not intend to be submitted.*" Fernandez & Hnos v. Rickert Rice Mills, 119 F. 2d 809, 815 (C.A. 1st Cir.). (Emphasis added.)

391; [6] Continental Milling & Feed Co. v. Doughnut Corp., 186 Md. 669, 48 A. 2d 447, 450; [7] Jacob v. Weisser, 207 Pa. 484, 56 A. 1065, 1067.[8] I believe that the Court today departs the established principles announced in these decisions.

Here, the employer operates a shop for the normal maintenance of its barges, but it is not equipped to make major repairs, and accordingly the employer has, from the beginning of its operations more than 19 years ago, contracted out its major work. During most, if not all, of this time the union has represented the employees in that unit. The District Court found that "[t]hroughout the successive labor agreements between these parties, including the present one, * * * [the union] has unsuccessfully sought to negotiate changes in the labor contract, and particularly during the negotiation of the present labor agreement, * * * which would have limited the right of the [employer] to continue the practice of contracting out such work." 168 Supp. F. 702, 704-705, 43 LRRM 2328.

[ARBITRATION CLAUSE]

The labor agreement involved here provides for arbitration of disputes respecting the interpretation and application of the agreement and, arguably, also some other things. But the first paragraph of the arbitration section says: [M]atters which are strictly a function of management shall not be subject to arbitration under this section." Although acquiescing for 19 years in the employer's interpretation that contracting out work was "strictly a function of management," and having repeatedly

---

[6] In this leading case, Judge, later Mr. Justice, Cardozo said:

"This question is one of intention, to be ascertained by the same tests that are applied to contracts generally. * * * No one is under a duty to resort to these conventional tribunals, however helpful their processes, *except to the extent that he has signified his willingness.* Our own favor or disfavor of the cause of arbitration is not to count as a factor in the appraisal of the thought of others." Marchant v. Mead-Morrison Mfg. Co., 252 N.Y. 284, 299, 169 N.E. 386, 391. (Emphasis added.)

[7] In this case, the Court, after quoting Judge Cardozo's language in Marchant, supra, saying that "the question is one of intention," said:

"Sound policy demands that the terms of an arbitration *must not be strained to discover power to pass upon matters in dispute, but the terms must be clear and unmistakable to oust the jurisdiction of the Court, for trial by jury cannot be taken away in any case merely by implication.*" Continental Milling & Feed Co. v. Doughnut Corp., 186 Md. 669, 676, 48 A 2d 447, 450. (Emphasis added.)

[8] "But, under any circumstances, before the decision of an arbitrator can be held final and conclusive, it must appear, as was said in Chandley Bros. v. Cambridge Springs, 200 Pa. 230, 49 Atl. 772, *that power to pass upon the subject-matter is clearly given to him. 'The terms of the agreement are not to be strained to discover it. They must be clear and unmistakable to oust the jurisdiction of the courts; for trial by jury cannot be taken away by implication merely in any case.'*" Jacob v. Weisser, 207 Pa. 484, 489, 5 A. 1065, 107. (Emphasis added.)

tried—particularly in the negotiation of the agreement involved here—
but unsuccessfully, to induce the employer to agree to a covenant that
would prohibit it from contracting out work, the union, after having
agreed to and signed the contract involved, presented a "grievance" on
the ground that the employer's contracting out work, at a time when
some employees in the unit were laid off for lack of work, constituted a
partial "lockout" of employees in violation of the anti-lockout provision
of the agreement.

Being unable to persuade the employer to agree to cease contracting
out work or to agree to arbitrate the "grievance," the union brought
this action in the District Court, under § 301 of the Labor Management
Relations Act, 29 U.S.C. § 185, for a decree compelling the employer to
submit the "grievance" to arbitration. The District Court, holding that
the contracting out of work was, and over a long course of dealings had
been interpreted and understood by the parties to be "strictly a function
of management," and was therefore specifically excluded from arbitration by the terms of the contract, denied the relief prayed, 168 F. Supp.
702, 43 LRRM 2328. The Court of Appeals affirmed, 269 F. 2d 633, 44
LRRM 2567, and we granted certiorari. 361 U.S. 912.

The Court now reverses the judgment of the Court of Appeals. It
holds that the arbitrator's source of law is "not confined to the express
provisions of the contract," that arbitration should be ordered "unless
it may be said with positive assurance that the arbitration clause is not
susceptible to an interpretation that covers the asserted dispute," that
"[d]oubts [of arbitrability] should be resolved in favor of coverage,"
and that when, as here, "a no-strike clause is included in the agreement,
then * * * everything that management does is subject to [arbitration]."
I understand the Court thus to hold that the arbitrators are not confined
to the express provisions of the contract, that arbitration is to be ordered
unless it may be said with positive assurance that arbitration of a particular dispute is excluded by the contract, that doubts of arbitrability
are to be resolved in favor of arbitration, and that when, as here, the
contract contains a no-strike clause, everything that management does is
subject to arbitration.

[STRANGE DOCTRINE]

This is an entirely new and strange doctrine to me. I suggest, with
deference, that it departs both the contract of the parties and the controlling decisions of this Court. I find nothing in the contract that purports to confer upon arbitrators any such general breadth of private
judicial power. The Court cites no legislative or judicial authority that
creates for or gives to arbitrators such broad general powers. And I

respectfully submit that today's decision cannot be squared with the statement of Judge, later Mr. Justice, Cardozo in Marchant that "no one is under a duty to resort to these conventional tribunals, however helpful their process, *except to the extent that he has signified his willingness.* Our own favor or disfavor of the cause of arbitration is not to count as a factor in the appraisal of the thoughts of others," 252 N.Y., at 299, 169 N.E., at 391 (emphasis added); nor with his statement in that case that "[t]he question is one of intention, to be ascertained by the same tests that are applied to contracts generally," id., nor with this Court's statement in Moorman, "that the intention of the parties to submit their contractual disputes to final determination outside the courts *should be made manifest by plain language,*" 338 U.S., at 462 (emphasis added); nor with this Court's statement in Hensey that: "To make such [an arbitrator's] certificate conclusive *requires plain language in the contract. It is not to be implied.*" 205 U.S. at 309. (Emphasis added.) "A party is never required to submit to arbitration any question which he has not agreed so to submit, and *contracts providing for arbitration will be carefully construed in order not to force a party to submit to arbitration a question which he did not intend to be submitted.*" Fernandez & Hnos v. Ricket Rice Mills, supra, 119 F. 2d at 815 (C.A. 1st Cir). (Emphasis added.)

With respect, I submit that there is nothing in the contract here to indicate that the employer "signified [its] willingness" (Marchant, supra, at 391) to submit to arbitrators whether it must cease contracting out work. Certainly no such intention is "made manifest by plain language" (Moorman, supra, at 462), as the law "requires," because such consent "is not to be implied." (Hensey, supra, at 309). To the contrary, the parties by their conduct over many years interpreted the contracting out of major repair work to be "strictly a function of management," and if, as the concurring opinion suggests, the words of the contract can "be understood only by reference to the background which gave rise to their inclusion," then the interpretation given by the parties over 19 years to the phrase "matters which are strictly a function of management" should logically have some significance here. By their contract, the parties agreed that "matters which are strictly a function of management shall not be subject to arbitration." The union over the course of many years repeatedly tried to induce the employer to agree to a covenant prohibiting the contracting out of work, but was never successful. The union again made such an effort in negotiating the very contract involved here, and, failing of success, signed the contract, knowing, of course, that it did not contain any such covenant, but that, to the contrary, it contained, just as had the former contracts, a covenant that "matters which are strictly a function of management shall not be subject to arbitration." Does not this show that, instead of signifying a willingness to submit to arbitration the matter of whether the employer might continue to contract out work, the parties fairly agreed to exclude at least that matter from arbitration? Surely it cannot be said that the parties agreed to such a submission by any "plain language." Moorman, supra, at 462, and Hensey, supra, at 309. Does not then the Court's opinion compel the employer "to submit to arbitration [a] question which [it] has not agreed so to submit"? (Fernandez & Hnos, supra, at 815.)

[JUDICIAL QUESTION]

Surely the question whether a particular subject or class of subjects are or are not made arbitrable by a contract is a judicial question, and if, as the concurring opinion suggests, "the Court may conclude that [the contract] commits to arbitration any [subject or class of subjects]," it may likewise conclude that the contract does not commit such subject or class of subjects to arbitration, and "[w]ith that finding the Court will have exhausted its function" no more nor less by denying arbitration than by ordering it. Here the District Court found, and the Court of Appeals approved its finding, that by the terms of the contract, as interpreted by the parties over 19 years, the contracting out of work was "strictly a function of management" and "not subject to arbitration." That finding, I think, should be accepted here. Acceptance of it requires affirmance of the judgment.

I agree with the Court that courts have no proper concern with the "merits" of claims which by contract the parties have agreed to submit to the exclusive jurisdiction of arbitrators. But the question is one of jurisdiction. Neither may entrench upon the jurisdiction of the other. The test is: Did the parties in their contract "manifest by plain language" (Moorman, supra, at 462) their willingness to submit the issue in controversy to arbitrators? If they did, then the arbitrators have exclusive jurisdiction of it, and the courts, absent fraud or the like, must respect that exclusive jurisdiction and cannot interfere. But if they did not, then the courts must exercise their jurisdiction, when properly invoked, to protect the citizen against the attempted use by arbitrators of pretended powers actually never conferred. That question always is, and from its very nature must be, a judicial one. Such was the question presented to the District Court and the Court of Appeals here. They found the jurisdictional facts, properly applied the settled law to those facts, and correctly decided the case. I would therefore affirm the judgment.

STEELWORKERS v. ENTERPRISE
WHEEL & CAR CORP.

Supreme Court of the United States

UNITED STEELWORKERS OF AMERICA v. ENTERPRISE
WHEEL AND CAR CORPORATION, No. 538, June 20, 1960

Full Text of Opinion

Mr. Justice DOUGLAS delivered the opinion of the Court.

Petitioner union and respondent during the period relevant here had a collective bargaining agreement which provided that any differences "as to the meaning and application" of the agreement should be submitted to arbitration and that the arbitrator's decision "shall be final and binding on the parties." Special provisions were included concerning the suspension and discharge of employees. The agreement stated:

"Should it be determined by the Company or by an arbitrator in accordance with the grievance procedure that the employee has been suspended unjustly or discharged in violation of the provisions of this Agreement, the Company shall reinstate the employee and pay full compensation at the employee's regular rate of pay for the time lost."

The agreement also provided:

" * * * It is understood and agreed that neither party will institute *civil suits or legal proceedings* against the other for alleged violation of any of the provisions of this labor contract; instead all disputes will be settled in the manner outlined in this Article III—Adjustment of Grievances."

[FACTS OF CASE]

A group of employees left their jobs in protest against the discharge of one employee. A union official advised them at once to return to work. An official of respondent at their request gave them permission and then rescinded it. The next day they were told they did not have a job any more "until this thing was settled one way or the other."

A grievance was filed; and when respondent finally refused to arbitrate, this suit was brought for specific enforcement of the arbitration provisions of the agreement. The District Court ordered arbitration. The arbitrator found that the discharge of the men was not justified, though their conduct, he said, was improper. In his view the facts warranted at most a suspension of the men for 10 days each. After their discharge and before the arbitration award the collective bargaining agreement had expired. The union, however, continued to represent the workers at the plant. The arbitrator rejected the contention that expiration of the agreement barred reinstatement of the employees. He held that the provision of the agreement above quoted imposed an unconditional obligation on the employer. He awarded reinstatement with back pay, minus pay for a 10-day suspension and such sums as these employees received from other employment.

Respondent refused to comply with the award. Petitioner moved the District Court for enforcement. The District Court directed respondent to comply. 168 F. Supp. 308, 43 LRRM 2291. The Court of Appeals, while agreeing that the District Court had jurisdiction to enforce an arbitration award under a collective bargaining agreement,[1] held that the failure of the award to specify the amounts to be deducted from the back pay rendered the award unenforceable. That defect, it agreed could be remedied by requiring the parties to complete the arbitration. It went on to hold, however, that an award for back pay subsequent to the date of termination of the collective bargaining agreement could not be enforced. It also held that the requirement for reinstatement of the discharged employees was likewise unenforceable because the collective agreement had expired. 269 F. 2d 327, 44 LRRM 2349.

[MERITS OF AWARDS]

The refusal of courts to review the merits of an arbitratiton award is the proper approach to arbitration under collective bargaining agreements. The federal policy of settling labor disputes by arbitration would be undermined if courts had the final say on the merits of the awards. As we stated in United Steelworkers of America v. Warrior & Gulf Navigation Co., ante, p. ——, 46 LRRM 2416, decided this day, the arbitrators under these collective agreements are indispensable agencies in a continuous collective bargaining process. They sit to settle disputes at the plant level—disputes that require for their solution knowledge of the custom and practices of a particular factory or of a particular industry as reflected in particular agreements.[2]

---

[1] See Textile Workers v. Cone Mills Corp., 268 F. 2d 920 (C.A. 4th Cir.).

[2] "Persons unfamiliar with mills and factories—farmers or professors, for example— often remark upon visiting them that they seem like another world. This is particularly true if, as in the steel industry, both tradition and technology have strongly and uniquely molded the ways men think and act when at work. The newly hired employee, the 'green hand,' is gradually initiated into what amounts to a miniature society. There he finds himself in a strange environment that assaults his senses with unusual sounds and smells and often with different 'weather conditions' such as sudden drafts of heat, cold, or humidity. He discovers that the society of which he only gradually becomes a part has of course a formal government of its own—the rules which management and the union have laid down—but that it also differs from or parallels the world outside in social classes, folklore, ritual, and traditions.

"Under the process in the old mills a very real 'miniature society' has grown up, and

When an arbitrator is commissioned to interpret and apply the collective bargaining agreement, he is to bring his informed judgment to bear in order to reach a fair solution of a problem. This is especially true when it comes to formulating remedies. There the need is for flexibility in meeting a wide variety of situations. The draftsmen may never have thought of what specific remedy should be awarded to meet a particular contingency. Nevertheless, an arbitrator is confined to interpretation and application of the collective bargaining agreement; he does not sit to dispense his own brand of industrial justice. He may of course look for guidance from many sources, yet his award is legitimate only so long as it draws its essence from the collective bargaining agreement. When the arbitrator's words manifest an infidelity to this obligation, courts have no choice but to refuse enforcement of the award.

[OPINION OF ARBITRATOR]

The opinion of the arbitrator in this case, as it bears upon the award of back pay beyond the date of the agreement's expiration and reinstatement, is ambiguous. It may be read as based solely upon the arbitrator's view of the requirements of enacted legislation, which would mean that he exceeded the scope of the submission. Or it may be read as embodying a construction of the agreement itself, perhaps with the arbitrator looking to "the law" for help in determining the sense of the agreement. A mere ambiguity in the opinion accompanying an award, which permits the inference that the arbitrator may have exceeded his authority, is not a reason for refusing to enforce the award. Arbitrators have no obligation to the court to give their reasons for an award. To require opinions [3] free of ambiguity may lead arbitrators to play it safe by writing no supporting opinions. This would be undesirable for a well reasoned opinion tends to engender confidence in the integrity of the process and aids in clarifying the underlying agreement. Moreover, we see no reason to assume that this arbitrator has abused the trust the parties confided in him and has not stayed within the areas marked out for his consideration. It is not apparent that he went beyond the submission. The Court of Appeal's opinion refusing to enforce the reinstatement and partial back pay portions of the award was not based upon any finding that the arbitrator did not premise his award on his con-

---

in important ways the technological revolution described in this case history shattered it. But a new society or work community was born immediately, though for a long time it developed slowly. As the old society was strongly molded by the *discontinuous* process of making pipe, so was the new one molded by the *continuous* process and strongly influenced by the characteristics of new highspeed automatic equipment." Walker, Life in the Automatic Factory, 3 Harv. Bus. Rev. 111, 117.

[3] See Jalet, "Judicial Review of Arbitration: The Judicial Attitude," 45 Cornell L. Q. 519, 522.

struction of the contract. It merely disagreed with the arbitrator's construction of it.

The collective bargaining agreement could have provided that if any of the employees were wrongfully discharged, the remedy would be reinstatement and back pay up to the date they were returned to work. Respondent's major argument seems to be that by applying correct principles of law to the interpretation of the collective bargaining agreement it can be determined that the agreement did not so provide, and that therefore the arbitrator's decision was not based upon the contract. The acceptance of this view would require courts, even under the standard arbitration clause, to review the merits of every construction of the contract. This plenary review by a court of the merits would make meaningless the provisions that the arbitrator's decision is final, for in reality it would almost never be final. This underlines the fundamental error which we have alluded to in United States Steelworkers of America v. American Manufacturing Co., ante, p. ——, 46 LRRM 2414, decided this day. As we there emphasized the question of interpretation of the collective bargaining agreement is a question for the arbitrator. It is the arbitrator's construction which was bargained for; and so far as the arbitrator's decision concerns construction of the contract, the courts have no business overruling him because their interpretation of the contract is different from his.

We agree with the Court of Appeals that the judgment of the District Court should be modified so that the amounts due the employees may be definitely determined by arbitration. In all other respects we think the judgment of the District Court should be affirmed. Accordingly, we reverse the judgment of the Court of Appeals, except for that modification, and remand the case to the District Court for proceedings in conformity with this opinion.

It is so ordered.

Mr. Justice FRANKFURTER concurs in the result.

Mr. Justice BLACK took no part in the consideration or decision of this case.

———

Dissenting Opinion

Mr. Justice WHITTAKER, dissenting.

Claiming that the employer's discharge on January 18, 1957, of 11 employees violated the provisions of its collective bargaining contract with the employer—covering the period beginning April 5, 1956, and ending April 5, 1957—the union sought and obtained arbitration, under the provisions of the contract, of the issues whether these employees had been discharged in violation of the agreement and, if so, should be ordered reinstated and awarded wages from the time of their wrongful discharge. In August 1957, more than four months after the collective agreement had expired, these issues were tried before and submitted to a Board of Arbitrators. On April 10, 1958, the arbitrators made their award, finding that the 11 employees had been discharged in violation of the agreement and ordering their reinstatement with back pay at their regular rates from a time 10 days after their discharge to the time of reinstatement. Over the employer's objection that the collective agreement and the submission under it did not authorize nor empower the arbitrators to award reinstatement or wages for any period after the date of expiration of the contract (April 5, 1957), the District Court ordered enforcement of the award. The Court of Appeals modified the judgment by eliminating the requirement that the employer reinstate the employees and pay them wages for the period *after* expiration of the collective agreement, and affirmed it in all other respects, 269 F. 2d 327, 44 LRRM 2349, and we granted certiorari, 361 U.S. 929.

That the propriety of the discharges, under the collective agreement, was arbitrable under the provisions of that agreement, even after its expiration, is not in issue. Nor is there any issue here as to the power of the arbitrators to award reinstatement status and back pay to the discharged employees to the date of expiration of the collective agreement. It is conceded, too, that the collective agreement expired by its terms on April 5, 1957, and was never extended or renewed.

The sole question here is whether the arbitrators exceeded the submission and their powers in awarding reinstatement and back pay for any period after expiration of the collective agreements. Like the Court of Appeals, I think they did. I find nothing in the collective agreement that purports to so authorize. Nor does the Court point to anything in the agreement that purports to do so. Indeed, the union does not contend that there is any such covenant in the contract. Doubtless all rights that accrued to the employees under the collective agreement during its term, and that were made arbitrable by its provisions, could be awarded to them by the arbitrators, even though the period of the agreement had ended. But surely no rights *accrued* to the employees under the agreement after it had expired. Save for the provisions of the collective agreement, and in the absence, as here, of any applicable rule of law or contrary covenant between the employer and the employees, the employer had the legal right to discharge the employees at will. The collective agreement, however, protected them against discharge, for specified reasons, during its continuation. But when that agreement expired, it did not continue to afford rights *in futuro* to the employees—as though still effective and governing. After the agreement expired the government status of these 11 employees was terminable at the will of the employer, as the Court of Appeals quite properly held, 269 F. 2d, at 331, 44LRRM 2349, and see Meadows v. Radio Industries, 222 F. 2d 347, 349, 36 LRRM 2147 (C.A. 7th Cir.); Atchison, T. & S. F. R. Co. v. Andrews, 211 F. 2d 264, 265 (C.A. 10th Cir.) ; Warden v. Hinds, 163 F. 201 (C.A. 4th Cir.), and the announced discharge of these 11 employees then became lawfully effective.

Once the contract expired, no rights continued to accrue under it to the employees. Thereafter they had no contractual right to demand that the employer continue to employ them, and *a fortiori* the arbitrators did not have power to order the employer to do so; nor did the arbitrators have power to order the employer to pay wages to them after the date of termination of the contract, which was also the effective date of their discharges.

The judgment of the Court of Appeals, affirming so much of the award as required reinstatement of the 11 employees to employment status and payment of their wages until expiration of the contract, but not thereafter, seems to me to be indubitably correct, and I would affirm it.

———

Concurring Opinion

[To decisions in United Steelworkers v. American Mfg. Co.; United Steelworkers v. Warrior and Gulf Navigation Co.; and United Steelworkers v. Enterprise Wheel and Car Corp.]

Mr. Justice BRENNAN, with whom Mr. Justice HARLAN joins, concurring.

While I join the Court's opinions in Nos. 443, 360 and 538, I add a word in Nos. 443 and 360.

In each of these two cases the issue concerns the enforcement of but one promise—the promise to arbitrate in the context of an agreement dealing with a particular subject matter, the industrial relations between employers and employees. Other promises contained in the collective bargaining agreements are beside the point unless, by the very terms of the arbitration promise, they are made relevant to its interpretation. And I emphasize this, for the arbitration promise is itself a contract. The parties are free to make that promise as broad or as narrow as they wish for there is no compulsion in law requiring them to include any such promise in their agreement. The meaning of the arbitration promise is not to be found simply by reference to the dictionary definitions of the words the parties use, or by reference to the interpretation of commercial arbitration clauses. Words in a collective bargaining agreement, rightly viewed by the Court to be the charter instrument of a system of industrial self-government, like words in a statute, are to be understood only by reference to the background which gave rise to their inclusion. The Court therefore avoids the prescription of inflexible rules for the enforcement of arbitration promises. Guidance is given by identifying the various considerations which a court should take into account when construing a particular clause—considerations of the milieu in which the clause is negotiated and of the national labor policy. It is particularly underscored that the arbitral process in collective bargaining presupposes that the parties wanted the informed judgment of an arbitrator, precisely for the reason that judges cannot provide it. Therefore, a court asked to enforce a promise to arbitrate should ordinarily refrain from involving itself in the interpretation of the substantive provisions of the contract.

[QUESTION FOR COURT]

To be sure, since arbitration is a creature of contract, a court must always inquire, when a party seeks to invoke its aid to force a reluctant party to the arbitration table, whether the parties have agreed to arbitrate the particular dispute. In this sense, the question of whether a dispute is "arbitrable" is inescapably for the court.

On examining the arbitration clause, the court may conclude that it commits to arbitration any "dispute, difference, disagreement, or controversy of any nature or character." With that finding the court will have exhausted its function, except to order the reluctant party to arbitration. Similarly, although the arbitrator may be empowered only to interpret and apply the contract, the parties may have provided that any dispute as to whether a particular claim is within the arbitration clause is itself for the arbitrator. Again the court, without more, must send any dispute to the arbitrator, for the parties have agreed that the construction of the arbitration promise itself is for the arbitrator, and the reluctant party has breached his promise by refusing to submit the dispute to arbitration.

[AMERICAN CASE]

In American, the Court deals with a request to enforce the "standard" form of arbitration clause, one that provides for the arbitration of "any disputes, misunderstandings, differences or grievances arising between the parties as to the meaning, interpretation and application of this agreement. * * *" Since the arbitration clause itself is part of the agreement, it might be argued that a dispute as to the meaning of that clause is for the arbitrator. But the Court rejects this position, saying that the threshold question, the meaning of the arbitration clause itself, is for the judge unless the parties clearly state to the contrary. However, the Court finds that the meaning of that "standard" clause is simply that the parties have agreed to arbitrate any dispute which the moving party asserts to involve construction of the substantive provisions of the contract, because such a dispute necessarily does involve such a construction.

[WARRIOR CASE]

The issue in the Warrior case is essentially no different from that in American, that is, it is whether the company agreed to arbitrate a particular grievance. In contrast to American, however, the arbitration promise here excludes a particular area from arbitration — "matters which are strictly a function of management." Because the arbitration promise is different, the scope of the court's inquiry may be broader. Here, a court may be required to examine the substantive provisions of the contract to ascertain whether the parties have provided that contracting out shall be a "function of management." If a court may delve into the merits to the extent of inquiring whether the parties have expressly agreed whether or not contracting-out was a "function of management," why was it error for the lower court here to evaluate the evidence of bargaining history for the same purpose? Neat logical distinctions do not provide the answer. The Court rightly concludes that appropriate regard for the national labor policy and the special factors relevant to the labor arbitral process, admonish that judicial inquiry into the merits of this grievance should be limited to the search for an explicit provision which brings the grievance under the cover of the exclusion clause since "the exclusion clause is vague and arbitration clause quite broad." The hazard of going further into the merits is amply demonstrated by what the courts below did. On the basis of inconclusive evidence, those courts found that Warrior was in no way limited by any implied covenants of good faith and fair dealing from contracting out as it pleased—which would necessarily mean that Warrior was free completely to destroy the collective bargaining agreement by contracting out all the work.

The very ambiguity of the Warrior exclusion clause suggests that the parties were generally more concerned with having an arbitrator render decisions as to the meaning of the contract than they were in restricting the arbitrator's jurisdiction. The case might of course be otherwise were the arbitration clause very narrow, or the exclusion clause quite specific, for the inference might then be permissible that the parties had manifested a greater interest in confining the arbitrator; the presumption of arbitrability would then not have the same force and the Court would be somewhat freer to examine into the merits.

The Court makes reference to an arbitration clause being the *quid pro quo* for a non-strike clause. I do not understand the Court to mean that the application of the principles announced today depends upon the presence of a no-strike clause in the agreement.

Mr. Justice FRANKFURTER joins these observations.

BRASS WORKERS UNION v. AMERICAN BRASS CO.

U.S. Court of Appeals,
Seventh Circuit (Chicago)

Brass and Copper Workers Federal Labor Union No. 19322, AFL-CIO, v. American Brass Company, etc., No. 12683, December 22, 1959.

Full Text of Opinion

HASTINGS, Chief Judge:—This is an action for specific performance under § 301 of the National Labor Relations Act, 29 U.S.C.A. 185, to compel arbitration under the relevant section of a collective bargaining agreement between the parties. The District Court sustained defendant's motion to dismiss plaintiff's complaint on the merits, and this appeal followed.

[ARBITRATION CLAUSES]

Appellant Brass and Copper Workers Federal Labor Union No. 19322, AFL-CIO (Union), and appellee American Brass Company, Kenosha Division, a Subsidiary of Anaconda Copper Company (Company) entered into an Amended Pension Plan Agreement and a Collective Bargaining Agreement (Agreement). The latter Agreement provided for arbitration under two separate sections. Article VII of the Agreement, entitled "Grievance Procedure," provided for a series of "steps" to be followed in the procedure of adjusting "any complaint, controversy or grievance" involving the "terms" of the Agreement. After conferences between the Company and Union at successively higher levels, provision was made for a joint or unilateral request for the intervention of the Federal Mediation and Conciliation Service (Mediation Service). Article VII expressly retained for both parties the right of arbitration in the case of discharges for cause or disciplinary layoffs, but such requests were required to be made "in writing *within ten (10) days after the Company's final answer in writing to the Union.*" (Emphasis added.)

Article VIII of the Agreement, entitled "Arbitration," provided for arbitratiton of "any dispute" involving "the interpretation or application of any part of this Agreement which cannot be settled between the parties." This article also specified a time limit for submission to arbitration of "ten (10) days following the date when it is determined that the parties cannot agree." The Article further required that the issues for decision be set forth in writing and that arbitrators confine their decision to such issues.

Thus both articles provided that arbitration must be requested within ten days as above set out. The contract did not, as such, indicate whether a court or an arbitrator should determine that the parties had complied with this requirement.

Both the Pension Plan and the Collective Bargaining Agreement were in effect on April 1, 1955, when the Company compulsorily retired all employees who were then 69 years of age or older. Such employees were not eligible for pensions under the Pension Plan [1] because of insufficient service with the Company.

On April 4, 1955, the Union orally and in writing [2] protested the compulsory retirement of the non-pensioners, complaining that such retirement constituted discharges without "cause," contrary to the provisions of the collective bargaining agreement and requested reinstatement and reimbursement for any loss suffered by reason of the compulsory retirement. The Company refused to reinstate the employees; it never gave a written answer to the Union's letter of April 4th.

On April 12, 1955, the Union wrote the Company as follows:

"In accordance with Article VII Section 4 lines 199 to 202 we request that the Company join with us in submitting the question of illegal discharge of employees mentioned in our communication to you under date of April 4, 1955, to the U.S. Department of Conciliation for disposal.

"Please advise at your convenience."

---

[1] The Pension Plan Agreement provided for the termination of the eligible employee's services following his sixty-eighth birthday, unless written permission was given to continue service beyond that date. On January 1, 1955, Company had retired all workers eligible under the Pension Plan.

[2] "In accordance with the Agreement now in effect between the American Brass Company and Local No. 19322, F.L.U.-A.F.L., the Union protests the illegal discharge of certain employees, listed in your communication to the Union under date of February 14, 1955, because of age. We further request reinstatement of said employees with all rights restored and retroactive pay for time lost because of such illegal discharge." (Relevant section of Union's letter.)

The Company's reply of April 14, 1955 was as follows:

"We acknowledge receipt of your communication of April 12, 1955 wherein you request that the Company join you in seeking the services of the U.S. Department of Conciliation.

"The Company does not consider that the retirement of certain employees referred to in your letter of April 4, 1955 to be illegal discharges and consequently cannot join you in your request."

After the Company's refusal to join in a mutual request to submit the grievance to the Mediation Service, the Union did not immediately request arbitration, but made a unilateral request for the Mediation Service to intervene.

On May 23, 1955, Virgil H. Burtz, a Commissioner of the Mediation Service, after having conferred with the Company, informed the Union that "very little, if anything, could be gained by a joint conference with one of our Commissioners present, as both parties' positions are firm" and that the parties were "free to proceed with arbitration in this matter."

On June 6, 1955, thirteen days after receipt of Burtz's letter, the Union requested arbitration of the discharges in the following letter:

"In accordance with Section 4 of Article VII the Union has contacted the Federal Mediation & Conciliation Service requesting that they mediate the dispute between the American Brass Company and Local No. 19322 regarding the discharge of employees 68 years of age and over. We have been advised that they are unable to mediate said dispute at this time. We are requesting that in accordance with the terms of our agreement that this question be submitted to arbitration. Please advise."

No written reply was ever received to this letter. On August 7, 1957, the Union instituted this action to compel arbitration of the dispute.

[CONFLICTING CONTENTIONS]

In the action below, the parties conceded the substantive arbitrability of the discharge (i.e., that the dispute is the type that the parties had agreed to arbitrate), but the Company contended that the merits of the case could not be reached because the Union had not followed the *procedural* requirements of the collective bargaining agreement. Specifically, the Company contended that the Union had not (as required by the Agreement) filed its request to arbitrate within ten days after the receipt of the Company's "final answer" of April 14, 1955. The Union argued that its filing was timely, or at least, that there was no prejudice even though the request for arbitration was filed delinquently. This conflict obviously required an interpretation of the contract.

But there was further conflict between the parties regarding *who* should resolve this problem. The Company stated that it was the responsibility of the court, in a suit for specific performance, to determine whether the Company had *broken its promise* to arbitrate. This determination must include not only the issue of whether the Company had agreed to arbitrate the subject matter (substantive arbitrability) but also whether the Union had complied with the agreed procedure to bring the grievance to arbitration (procedural arbitrability). The Union, however, contended that the latter matter should be determined by the arbitrator himself prior to his consideration of the merits.

[THEORY OF COURT BELOW]

The District Court held that under the contract in question, the issue of procedural compliance necessary to bring the matter before the arbitrator was itself arbitrable under Article VIII as an "interpretation * * * of any term of the agreement," but that since the dispute was not negotiated below and *formally* made a part of the grievance procedure, it was not an arbitrable dispute properly subject to a decree for specific performance.

Since the dispute over procedural arbitrability had not been formally processed through the grievance procedure, the trial court could find no inference from the Agreement that the parties intended this issue to be submitted to the arbitrator. Relying on the case of Boston Mutual Life Ins. Co. v. Insurance Agents' Int. Un. 1 Cir. 258 F.2d 516, (1958), the court determined the issue was one for it to decide. Proceeding with such determination and Analysis of the Agreement, it held that under the procedure of Article VII, the Union must consider the Company's letter of April 14, 1955, as a "final answer." But even assuming the Union was proceeding under Article VIII (although its letter of June 6 mentioned only Article VII), Burtz's letter of May 23 was held to be a "final answer," and the request for arbitration was not made until thirteen days later. Since this was in excess of the time limit stated in "unambiguous language" in the Agreement, the court refused to grant specific performance, holding that the Union "has lost its rights to enforcement of the arbitration promise by non-compliance."

This appeal is based on dual grounds, first, that the issue of compliance with the Agreement is for the arbitrator to decide, and second, if for the court, that the court below erred in its determination of the issues under the Agreement.

[PROCEDURAL ARBITRABILITY]

The question of procedural arbitrability is therefore drawn in sharp terms. The necessity for determining this issue flows, essentially, from the case of Textile Workers v. Lincoln Mills, 353 U.S. 448 (1957), in which the court held that promises to arbitrate were specifically enforceable under § 301 of the Taft-Hartley Act and that federal rules of decision controlled cases under this section. Since there was no extensive residuum of federal law except the express provisions of the Taft-Hartley Act on this subject, the Court charged the judiciary to fashion a federal common law on a case-by-case basis. In exercising this traditional judicial function, courts were to be guided by the purposes of national labor legislation and could absorb state rules of decision as federal law when such were consistent with the goals of national labor policy.

Subsequent to the holding that § 301 provides a forum for a party to bring an action to compel arbitration under a collective bargaining agreement, federal courts have been faced with the problem of determining when it is proper to order arbitration. The initial problem involved substantive arbitrability, which in turn, required a delineation of the power and responsibility of judges and arbitrators. It is obvious that an arbitrator's range of decision is necessarily restricted by a court's prior determination whether the parties had agreed to arbitrate the subject matter of the dispute.

In each case it is a collective bargaining agreement that the court must interpret. In certain instances the parties expressly indicate that arbitrability is for the courts. See Local 201, etc. v. General Electric Company, 1 Cir., 262 F.2d 265 (1959). Many times parties voluntarily submit arbitrability to the arbitrators.[3] The difficult case arises, as here, when the agreement does not expressly indicate who should decide this issue.

It is now well-settled that issues of substantive arbitrability are for the courts to determine. The keystone decision was Local No. 149, etc. v. General Electric Company, 1 Cir., 250 F.2d 922 (1957), cert. denied 356 U.S. 938 (1958). Chief Judge Magruder there concluded that when one of the parties to a collective bargaining agreement appears before a court requesting a decree ordering specific performance of a contract to arbitrate, the court "has the inescapable obligation to determine as a preliminary matter that the defendant has contracted to refer such issue to arbitration, and has broken this promise." Id. at 927.[4]

---

[3] A survey conducted by the American Arbitration Association of 1,728 grievances in 1954 shows that the issue of arbitrability was raised in a total of 133 cases, or 7.7%. In 41 of these cases, arbitrability was the sole issue. Only three of 1,183 cases studied involved court action to compel specific performance of the promise to arbitrate. American Arbitration Association, Procedural and Substantive Aspects of Labor Management Relations.

[4] In addition, see New Bedford Defense Prod. Div. v. Local No. 1113, etc., 1 Cir., 258 F. 2d 222, 42 LRRM 2518 (1958) (rejecting the "Cutler-Hammer doctrine"); Engineers Ass'n. v. Sperry Gyroscope Co., etc., 2 Cir., 251 F. 2d 133 (1957); Lodge No. 12, etc. v. Cameron Iron Works, 5 Cir., 257 F. 2d 467 (1958); Refinery Employees Union v.

In this decision Chief Judge Magruder examined the contention of those commenters who urge that the issue of substantive arbitrability be left, in the first instance, for the arbitrator [5] But he concludes that these arguments are not controlling in the case where a party comes to the court for specific performance,[6] but are important and persuasive for the parties at the bargaining table in writing a contract which grants arbitrators wide scope in their decisions and even in expressly reserving such a determination for the arbitrator.[7]

Continental Oil Co., 5 Cir., 268 F. 2d 447 (1959); International Union, etc. v. Benton Harbor Mal. Ind., 6 Cir., 242 F. 2d 536 (1957) (pre-Lincoln Mills); American Lava Corp. v. Local Union No. 222, etc., 6 Cir., 250 F. 2d 137 (1958); United Steelworkers of America v. American Mfg. Co., 6 Cir., 264 F. 2d 624, 628 (1959) (holding that a "frivolous, patently baseless" grievance, although substantively arbitrable was not arbitrable under the agreement between the parties); Machinist Local 1912, etc. v. U.S. Potash Co., 10 Cir., 270 F. 2d 406 (1959).

[5] "We are aware of a viewpoint urged in responsible quarters that the interests of effective labor arbitration would best be served by committing to the arbitrator in the first instance the question of arbitrability, that is, the question whether there is any issue to be arbitrated under the collective bargaining agreement. It is said that a collective bargaining contract is a very special type of document, in respect of interpretation, as to which an arbitrator has certain advantages over a court, that a collective bargaining agreement, though embracing a multitude of terms covering numerous employees working at various tasks, cannot be expected to have pin-pointed each of many problems to be dealt with in relations between the management and the union; that the contract instead contains unexpressed assumptions that many procedures and practices will continue; that under the more simplified and speedy procedures of an arbitration, more evidence with regard to these unexpressed assumptions may be available, and an arbitrator may have the additional advantage of background knowledge derived from past experiences with the parties. Therefore it may be desirable in the first instance to have an arbitrator pass on the threshold question of arbitrability, instead of running the possible risk that a court, in the guise of ruling on this preliminary question of the jurisdiction of the arbitrator, may in effect make a ruling upon the merits of the asserted grievance. See Summers, 'Judicial Review of Labor Arbitration or Alice Through the Looking Glass.' Buffalo L. Rev. 1 (1952); Cox, 'Some Lawyers' Problems in Grievance Arbitration,' 40 Minn. L. Rev. 41 (1955); Clifton, 'Arbitration and Arbitrability,' 3d Annual Conference on Labor N.Y.U. 187 (1950). See also Greyhound Corp. v. Division 1384 of Amalgamated Association of Street, etc., Employees of America, 1954, 44 Wash. 2d 808, 271 P. 2d 689, 22 LA 555. See also an address by Professor Cox at the University of Cincinnati Conference on Labor Arbitration, November 14, 1957, entitled 'Current Problems in the Law of Grievance Arbitration.'" 250 F. 2d at 926, 41 LRRM 2247.

[6] A state case heavily relied upon by appellant here. Southwestern New Hampshire Transp. Co. v. Durham, — N.H. — 152 A. 2d 596 (1959), holds that procedural arbitrability is for the arbitrator to decide. This case, however, was an *appeal* from the prior ruling of arbitrators. It does not meet the core of the problem in an action to *compel* arbitration, in which the court has to determine how extensively it would examine whether the reluctant party had breached its promise to arbitrate.

[7] Local No. 149 was based both on an independent analysis of the court's responsibility under § 301 and on the practice under the United States Arbitration Act. In a prior decision to Lincoln Mills, Local 205, etc. v. General Electric Company, 1 Cir., 233 F. 2d 85, 101 (1956), the court had determined a similar case under the Arbitration Act. On certiorari, in an opinion accompanying Lincoln Mills, General Electric Co. v. Local 205, 353 U.S. 547 (1957), the Court affirmed the judgment, but stated that it followed "a different path * * * [to] the same result." 353 U.S. at 548.

In the sole post-Lincoln Mills case under § 301 which has involved procedural arbitrability, Boston Mutual Life Insurance Co. v. Insurance Agents' Int. Un., 1 Cir., 258 F.2d 516 (1958), Chief Judge Magruder held that the court was unwilling to "whittle away" the holding in Local No. 149 and determined that under the rationale of that case, procedural arbitrability is in the first instance, a matter for the courts to determine.[8]

In Boston Mutual, the employer requested a declaratory judgment that the union's grievance claim with respect to the discharge of an employee had not been submitted for arbitration within a reasonable time and was therefore not subject to arbitration. In his holding, Chief Judge Magruder again referred to the large body of opinion which argues that arbitrators should be given wide sway, but concludes this is relevant to the bargaining table, not to a decree for enforcement. He stated, however, that "practical considerations as to what would best promote effective labor arbitrations," id. at 517, might be an element in construing the scope of ambiguous language as to the matters sent to arbitration. However, the court concluded that the "inescapable obligation" of determining the issue of seasonable submission to arbitration was for the court,[9] and remanded for that consideration.[10]

We approve the rationale of the decision in Boston Mutual. In the case where a collective bargaining agreement gives no indication of the intended party to determine the issue of procedural arbitrability, it is, in the first instance, for the court to make this decision in a suit brought to compel arbitration. Accordingly, we hold that the district court was correct in considering this issue.

[REQUEST FOR ARBITRATION]

Further, having found that the district court properly considered the issue of procedural arbitrability, we find no error in its disposition of this case. Even considering the events most favorable to appellants (that the

---

[8] In a pre-Lincoln Mills case, decided under Pennsylvania law, the district court sent to the arbitrator the question of whether an alleged two-day violation of agreed procedure precluded bringing the action. The court stated, "Arbitration is here to stay, and particularly where the parties have elected to submit their differences to it, the courts should not try by hair-splitting decisions [to] hamstring its operation." Insurance Agents' Inter. Union v. Prudential Ins. Co., D.C.E.D. Pa., 122 F. Supp. 669, 872 (1954).

[9] Commentators have been critical of the result in Boston Mutual. See Gregory. The Law of the Collective Agreement, 57 Mich. L. Rev. 635, 638 (1959); Cox, Reflections Upon Labor Arbitration. 72 Harv. L. Rev. 1482, 1511 (1959).

[10] On remand, the district court held that the application for arbitration was made with due diligence, depending to a great degree on the fact that there was no substantial prejudice occasioned by the delay. Boston Mutual Life Ins. Co. v. Insurance Agents' Int. U., D. C. Mass., 171 F. Supp. 125 (1959).

letter of May 23 was the "final answer"), appellant's request for arbitration came too later under the terms of the Agreement, since it was made thirteen days after receipt of the final answer.

The judgment of the district court dismissing plaintiff's complaint on the merits is

Affirmed.

INDEX